THE HOME LOTS

OF THE

EARLY SETTLERS

OF THE

PROVIDENCE PLANTATIONS,

WITH NOTES AND PLATS.

BY

CHARLES WYMAN HOPKINS.

CLEARFIELD

Originally published
Providence, Rhode Island, 1886

Reprinted for
Clearfield Company by
Genealogical Publishing Co.
Baltimore, Maryland
1997, 2001, 2004, 2007

ISBN-13: 978-0-8063-4680-9
ISBN-10: 0-8063-4680-9

Made in the United States of America

TABLE OF CONTENTS.

ILLUSTRATIONS.

INTRODUCTION.

THE increasing interest in matters pertaining to the early history of Providence which the near approach of the two hundred and fiftieth anniversary of the settlement of the town has occasioned, induces the writer to present the following " PLAN OF THE HOME LOTS " of the early settlers of Providence, the founders of our Commonwealth and the ancestors of thousands of the citizens of Rhode Island. Such brief notes and extracts from the public records, concerning the persons and estates as are of general interest or will serve to illustrate or verify the Plan, have also been added.

Soon after the settlement of Providence in 1636, the territory included within the limits of the present Olney, Hope, Wickenden, North and South Main streets, comprising perhaps two hundred and seventy-five acres of land, was divided into "shares" or "home lots" of five acres each, more or less, extending from the " Towne Streete," now North and South Main streets, to " The Highway at the head of the lotts," now Hope street, and assigned to the proprietors and by many of them occupied as their homesteads.

For many years the location of a large number of these homesteads has remained unidentified.

Judge Staples, in the "Annals of Providence," pages 34 and 36, says: " With respect to the first division of land in 'the grand purchase of Providence' little can be gathered from the records." " The dividing lines between all these lots run east and west, and many of them may be traced by the walls and fences now [1843] standing. Several of these lots have never been transferred by deed."

Mr. Henry C. Dorr, in his interesting and valuable work, "The Planting and Growth of Providence," No. 15 of the series of "Rhode Island Historical Tracts," pages 17 and 18, states that "The early allotment of the homesteads has become involved in obscurity through the loss of the early documents of the town. We know not how soon the distribution was made, or the mode of proceeding."

The late Rev. Edwin M. Stone, the author of "Our French Allies," and other works relating to Rhode Island history, in "The Burning of Providence," an article published in the *Providence Journal,* April 10, 1876, writes as follows in regard to the location of the homesteads:

"Along the town street most of the population resided, with here and there a townsman living some distance from it. It is impossible to fix the exact location of each house, yet some spots may be pointed out."

"We have been at much pains to obtain accurate information concerning the home lots and residences of the first settlers of the town, and regret that we are at present unable to make it complete."

"It would be interesting to know the exact spot upon which each of the fifty-four proprietors built their dwellings." "If any of our antiquarian readers can throw further light upon the subject, or will correct any error in statement they may discover in the general narrative, we shall esteem the service a favor."

The "History of Warwick," by O. P. Fuller, page 47, locates the home lot of John Warner "near where the 'What Cheer' building now stands."

Other illustrations might be given. The foregoing are sufficient, however, to show the vague and indefinite character of the information which has for a long time prevailed concerning this subject. Not more than fifteen, perhaps, of the original fifty-two home lots have been definitely located, the remaining thirty or forty having become lost, apparently, in the mists of two centuries and a half. It is believed that a solution of this problem will be of interest and of practical use in tracing the titles and boundaries of the early estates of Providence.

The accompanying plan of the "Home Lots" is founded upon a record contained in a little book in the office of the City Clerk, Providence, dated 1660, and which contains a list of the "Home Lots," "beginning at Mile-End Cove." This record, torn in places, and partially obliterated by long use, bears evidence of having been carefully written by Roger Williams, and is reproduced in the appendix, at the close of this volume, for the purpose of preservation and for convenient reference.

In the preparation of this brief summary of the settlement at Providence, the writer has been materially aided by the kind suggestions of a number of gentlemen, too numerous to be mentioned by name, to all of whom he desires to express his sincere thanks for the assistance rendered.

The Parish Church at Gwinear, Cornwall, England.

From Photograph taken May, 1886, expressly for this work.

ROGER WILLIAMS

AND THE

SETTLEMENT AT PROVIDENCE.

THE purchase of the "lands and meadows upon the two fresh rivers," and the settlement at Providence, are themes intimately connected with the record of the lives of those men who, twice exiled from their homes, found at last an asylum upon the banks of the Moshassuck. The beautiful scene which lay spread out before them in all its native wildness, as they for the first time climbed the eastern hillside on that day in early summer, has been transformed as if by magic. They themselves have long since passed away, and in place of the forest, at first their only shelter, stands the fair City of Providence, with its thousands of happy homes, its hum of industry, and its temples of learning and of worship, far better memorials of its founders than

"Storied urn or animated bust."

Roger Williams, pre-eminent as the father and founder of the colony and the great apostle of religious liberty, was born of Welch parentage about the year 1600. In the register of the parish church at Gwinear, Cornwall, may be found the following record:

> "Anno do 1600
> "Roger the Second Sonne of William Williams a gent" was
> baptized the xxiiii[th] daie of Julye."

He was educated at Cambridge University, and chose the ministry for his profession. His liberal views, however, finding too narrow limits in those days of intolerance, forced him, in common with other persecuted Puritans, to seek an asylum in the wilds of America.

He arrived at Boston, with his wife, Mary,[1] on the fifth of February, 1630–1, and resumed his labors in the ministry. The General Court disapproving of his teachings, summoned him to reply to charges which finally resulted in his banishment.

About the middle of January, 1635–6, the Court having decided that Williams should be sent back to England, he hastily bade adieu to sympathizing friends, left his wife and two babes, the elder about two years of age, the younger but three months, and braving the bitter cold and deep snow of a New England winter, made his way through an unbroken wilderness to seek shelter and safety in the territory of the Narragansetts.

In a letter to his friend, Major Mason, dated Providence, June 22, 1670, he says:

> "When I was unkindly and unchristianly, as I believe, driven from my house, and land, and wife, and children, (in the midst of a New England winter, now about thirty-five years past,) at Salem, that ever-honored Governor, Mr. Winthrop, privately wrote to me to steer my course to the Narragansett Bay and Indians, for many high and heavenly and public ends, encouraging me, from the freeness of the place from any English claims or patents. I took his prudent motion as a hint and voice from God, and, waiving all other thoughts and motions, I steered my course from Salem—(though in winter-snow, which I feel yet)—unto these parts, wherein I may say *Peniel,* that is, I have seen the face of God."

---

1. Her maiden name is believed to have been Warnard. (See Knowles' Memoirs of Roger Williams, p. 31.)

Anno do 1600

Roger the Sonne of William williams ypton was
Baptized the xviij the Sone of July

He obtained from Ousamequin, also known as Massasoit, father of King Philip, a grant of land at Seekonk, on the east side of Pawtucket River, at a place formerly called " Manton's Neck," on the northern bank of the little cove which is the out-let of the Ten Mile River.

Here he was joined by some of his friends from Salem and began to "build and plant," but being kindly informed by his friend, Governor Winslow, that he was still within the bounds of the Plymouth Patent, he gave up his new resi-dence, and, in company with five companions, went down the river in a canoe, and nearing the western shore of the river, was greeted by the friendly salutation of the natives, "*What Cheer, Netop.*" Here they landed and exchanged greetings with the Indians. Re-embarking, they passed around the southerly point of land, now India and Fox Points, and proceeding up the Providence River disembarked at a place where they found a spring of water gushing from the hillside. This spot they selected for a home, and in grateful remembrance of " God's merciful kindness to him in his distress," the town thus founded, Roger Williams named PROVIDENCE.

This was in the spring or early summer of 1636, generally supposed to have been in the latter part of June.[1] The names of the five persons who accompanied Roger Williams at this time are William Harris, John Smith (the miller), Joshua Verin, Thomas Angell and Francis Wickes. These, with Mr. Williams, were the first settlers of Providence.

True to the principle which he had boldly advocated before his banishment, that the Indians were the rightful owners of the land, on the 24th of March, in the second year of the Plantation, Roger Williams procured from Canonicus and Miantonomi, sachems of the Narragansetts, the deed of lands purchased two years before.

1. Knowles' Mem. R. W., pp. 102–103; also, " When was Providence Founded?" in the *Providence Journal*, January 25, 1886; " The True Date of the Founding of Providence," in *Book Notes*, by Sidney S. Rider, Vol. 3, No. 26, p. 127; " Founding of Providence," in *Evening Telegram*, March 22, 1886.

The original deed is so dilapidated as to be partially illegible, but the Town Court caused approved copies to be recorded in the town records, and those copies, together with the action of the Court in regard to them, are as follows:

"The Seventh of the Twelfe Month 1658
    At our Towne Court;
    William Arnold of Pautuxet Came into
    this presant Court and did acknowledge
    That those two Coppies (to witt) of William
    Harrises & Thomas Olneys which hath these
    words in them as ffolloweth, are the true
    words of that writeing Called the towne Evi-
    -dence of Providence, And that which is want-
    -ing in the now writeing called the towne Evi-
    -dence, which agreeth not with those two Coppies
    was torne by accident in his house at Pautuxett.

        A true Coppye of the Towne Evidence,
          as followeth.

Att Nanhiggansick, The 24th of the first Month
Comonly called March in the Second yeare of our
plantation, or planting at Moshausick, or
Providence.
Memorandum, That wee Caunanicusse and
Meiuuantunnomu the two chiefe Sachims
of Nanheggansuck, haveing Two yeares
since sold unto Roger Williams the lands & mead-
-dowes upon the two fresh Rivers called mow-
-shausuck & wanasquatuckett, doe now by these
presents Establish & Confirme the bounds of those
lands from the Rivers & ffields of Pautuckett, The
great hill of Neotaconkonitt on the Norwest and

... monts
... yeare of
... Mooshausick or Providence
... canonicus & Miantunno
... ... of Mashiggonuck
... yeare ... sold unto ... Mr William
... downe upon this ... first now
... ... wanasquatuckqut ...
... ... establish & Conforme
... bound ... from y[e] river ...
... ... great hill of Nota...
... ... Nowoest ... the ...

... we have ...

... y[e] ...   Caunounicus

... Josiash

                                              Miantunnomy

... ... at ... by each ...
... at know ... at ...
... ... about ... w[th] ...
... ... fere ...

the towne of Mashapauge on the west.
As also in Consideration of the many Kindness-
-es & services he hath continually done for us both
with our friends of Massachusett, as also at Quinitik-
-ticutt, And Apaum or Plimouth, wee doe freely
Give unto him all that land from those Rivers
Reaching to Pautuxett River, as also the Grasse
& meaddowes upon Pautuxett River. In witnes
where of wee haue hereunto set our hands in the
presence of

The marke ⌣ Caunanicusse

The mark of ⊙ Soatash

The marke of ↰ Assotemewett

of

The marke of ⚡ Meiantenomu

1639, Memorandum. 3. month. 9. day. This was all againe
confirmed by Miantenomu he acknowledged this his act
and hand up the streame of Pautuckett & Pautuxett
without limmets wee might have for our use of Cattell.
Wittnes hereof   ROGER WILLIAMS
                                   BENEDICT ARNOLD.

Att A Towne metting March the 6ᵗ 1659. 60
    Tho: Olney Senʳ Moderator.

*   *   *   *   *

ffor as much as William Harris hath this day
desired of the Towne that he might have the
Towne Evidence downe to Newport haveing
ocation to use it at the Court
    It is therefore granted that the clarke shall
delivere the said Evidence unto the said
William Harris; and the said William Harris shall

2

deliver the said Evidence unto the clarke again
saffely in convenient season as the Towne
shall see meette:

* * * * *

The Enrolement of the wrighting Called the
Towne Evidence after it was defaced; (as ffolloweth)

Att Nanhiggansick; the 24th of the first Month Comonly called
March the 2nd yeare of our plantation, or planting at
Moshosick, or providence,
Memorandum, that wee Caunounicus, & Miantenomu y[e] 2 cheife
Sachims of Nanhiggansick having 2 yeares since Sold unto Roger
Williams y[e] landes & Meaddowes upon the 2 fresh Rivers called
Moshosick & wanasquatuckett doe Now by these presentes Establish, & confirme y[e] boundes of those landes from y[e] River & fieldes
of pautuckquitt, y[e] great hill of Neotaconckonett on y[e] Norwest,
& y[e] Towne of Mashappauge on y[e] West.
in wittnesse where of wee have here unto Sett our handes

y[e] m[ke] of ⌣ Caunounicus

in y[e] presence of

y[e] m[ke] of ⋏ Miantenomu

y[e] m[ke] ◯ of Soatash

y[e] m[ke] ⌒ of Asotemewitt

M[d] 3 Mont: 9 die this was all againe confirmed by Miantenomu
he acknowledged this his act and hand up the streame of pautuckett
and Pautuxett without limmetts we might have for our use of
Cattle wittnesse here of

BENEDICT

ROGER WILLIAMS: ARNOLD

Enroled Aprill y[e] 4th: 1662: p me Tho: Olney Jun[r]:
Towne Clerke.

This earliest deed upon the records of Providence, after the transfer by Roger Williams of equal rights to his associates, was, in 1659, confirmed "to the men of Providence and the men of Pawtuxet," by the sachems, successors of Canonicus and Miantonomi. These deeds of confirmation also extended the purchase "twenty full miles from a hill called Fox's hill," and more clearly defined the western bounds of the colony.

Of these lands, comprising the greater portion of the present County of Providence and a part of the County of Kent, Roger Williams was at first the sole purchaser and proprietor.

He asserts that "It is not true that I was employed by any, was supplied by any, or desired any to come with me into these parts." "My soul's desire was to do the natives good, and to that end to learn their language, (which I afterward printed,) and therefore desired not to be troubled with English company;" that out of pity he gave leave to several persons to come along in his company. He adds: "I mortgaged my house in Salem (worth some hundreds) for supplies to go through, and therefore was it a single business." He says that "It was by God's merciful assistance, I was the procurer of the purchase and not by means or payments, the natives being so shy and jealous that moneys could not do it, but by that language, acquaintance and favor with the natives, and other advantages which it pleased God to give me, and also bore the charges and venture of all the gratuities, which I gave to the great sachems, and other sachems round about us, and lay engaged for a loving and peaceable neighborhood with them to my great charge and travel."

Mr. Williams thus received a clear title to these lands, and might have retained them if he had so desired. Such, however, was not his purpose. He desired rather that the lands so purchased at his own expense might be "for a shelter for persons distressed for conscience," a colony founded upon civil freedom, where all might worship God according to the dictates of their own conscience.

Accordingly, soon after his purchase he executed the following deed, gener-
ously dividing the land equally among his associates, which had now increased to
twelve in number, "without reserving to himself," as he afterwards observed, "a
foot of land or an inch of voice more than to my servants and strangers."

Memorandum or "Initial Deed" from Roger Williams of the lands purchased
from Canonicus and Miantonomi:

"Memorandum, That I, R. W. having formerly purchased of Canonicus and
Miantonomi, this our situation or plantation of New Providence, viz. the two
fresh rivers Wonas. and Moosh. and the grounds and meadows thereupon, in consideration of £30 received from the inhabitants of said place, do freely and
fully, pass, grant and make over equal right and power of enjoying and disposing
the same grounds and lands unto my loving friends and neighbors, S W.
W A. T J. R C. J G. J T. W H. W C. T O. F W. R W. and E H.
and such others as the major part of us shall admit into the same fellowship of
vote with us. As also, I do freely, make and pass over equal right and power of
enjoying and disposing the said land and ground reaching from the aforesaid
rivers unto the great river Pawtuxett, with the grass and meadow thereupon,
which was so lately given and granted by the two aforesaid sachems to me. Witness my hand.   R. W."[1]

There was no date affixed to the above deed, and on the 22d of the 10th
month [Dec.], 1666, Roger Williams executed a second memorandum of his purchase from Canonicus and Miantonomi, as follows:

"The Enrollment of a Writing signed by Roger Williams as followeth:

"Providence, 8th of 8th Mon: 1638. (so called.)
"Memorandum, that I Roger Williams having formerly purchased of Cau-
nouinicus & Miantinomue, this our Situation, or Plantation of New Providence

---

1. From Staples' Annals of Providence, pp. 28-29.

Viz, the two fresh rivers Wanasquatuckett & Mooshausick and the ground & meadows thereupon, in consideration of thirty Pounds received from the Inhabitants of the said Place, do freely & fully pass, grant & make over equal right and power of enjoying & disposing the same grounds & lands unto my loving friends & neighbors, Stukely Westcott, Wm. Arnold, Thomas James, Robert Cole, John Greene, John Throckmorton, William Harris, William Carpenter, Tho: Olney, ffrancis Weston, Richard Waterman, Ezekiel Holliman and such others as the Major Part of us shall admit into the same fellowship of Vote with us. As also I do freely make and pass over equal right and power of enjoying and disposing of the lands and grounds reaching from the aforesaid rivers unto the great river Pawtuxett with the grass and meadows thereupon, which was so lately given and granted by the aforesaid Sachims to me. Witness my Hand,

ROGER WILLIAMS."

" Providence, 22ᵈ 10, 1666, (so called.)

"This Paper and Writing is a true Copy of a writing given by me about twenty-eight years since and differs not a tittle only so is dated as near as we could guess about the time and the names of men (written in a straight of time and haste) are here explained by me,

ROGER WILLIAMS.

" In the presence of us
   JOHN BROWNE,
   JOHN SAYLES,
   THOMAS HARRIS, Assistant."[1]

On the 20th of December, 1661, in compliance with a request of the proprietors of the town of Providence, Roger Williams executed the following deed in confirmation of the initial deed :

1. Deeds, &c., Trans., p. 190,

" Be it Knowne unto all men by these presentes, That I Roger Williams
of the Towne of Providence in the Narragansett Bay in New England having
in the Yeare one Thousand six hundred Thirtye ffoure And in the Yeare one
Thousand six hundred Thirtye ffive, had severall Treatyes with Counanicusse And
Miantenome, the Two chiefe Sachims of the Narragansett; And in the End purchased of them the 𝕷𝖆𝖓𝖉𝖊𝖘 𝖆𝖓𝖉 𝕸𝖊𝖆𝖉𝖉𝖔𝖜𝖊𝖘 upon the Two ffresh Rivers called
Moshosick, And Wanasquatuckett The Two said Sachims having by A Deede
under theire handes, Two Yeares after the sale thereof Established, And Conffirmed
the Boundes of those 𝕷𝖆𝖓𝖉𝖊𝖘 ffrom the River And ffeildes of Pautuckett, the great
Hill of Neotaconkonitt on the Norwest And the Towne of Mashapaug on the
west; Notwithstanding, I had the frequent promise of Miantenomy (my Kind
freind) that It should not be Land that I should want about these Boundes mentioned, provided, that I satisffied the Indian; there inhabeting; I having made
Covenants of peaceable neighbourhood with all the Sachims, And Natives Round
about us, And having in A sence of God's mercifull Providence unto me in my
destresse, call the place Providence, I desired it might be for A shelter for persons
destressed for Conscience; I then considering the condition of Divers of my
destressed countrey men; I comunicated my said purchase unto my loving ffreindes,
John Throckmorton, William Arnold, William Harris, Stuckley Westcott, John
Greene Senior, Thomas Olney Senior, Richard Watermane And others, who then
desired to take Shelter here with me, And in Succession, unto so many others as
we Should Receive into the felloship, And Societye of injoyeing, And desposing
of the Said Purchase: And besides the ffirst that were admitted, our Towne
Recordes declare, that afterwards wee Received Chad Browne, William ffield,
Thomas Harris Senior, William Wickenden, Robert Williams, Grigorey Dexter,
and others as our Towne Booke declares: And whereas by Gode's Mercifull Assistance I was the procurer of the purchase not by monies nor payment, the Natives
being so shy, And jeloues that monies could not do it, but by that Language,
Aquaintance, And favour with the Natives, And other Advantages which it
pleased God to give me, And also bore the charges, And Venture of all the

Be it knowne unto all men by these presents, That I of Roger Williams of the Towne of providence in the
Narragansett Bay in New England, having in the yeare one thousand six hundred thirty fiue and in the
yeare one thousand six hundred thirty six had and obtayned of the two cheife Sachims of the Narraganset Cannanicus and Miantonomie the
vpon the two cheife Sachims of the Narragansett Bay... called Mooshasuck and in the End of ... and from the Landes and Meddowes
vse (Riuer Landes, two yeares after the sale thereof ... the two said Sachims summ of the Landes from the Riuer ... ... Boundes of the
And the Towne of Mishawaucke on the west ... ... the great Hill of ... heard on the more
mysting (said), that I Satisffied ... ... not so Land, that I should want about ... ... the neighbourhood
with all the Sachims, the natiues Round about us, the ... ... made Couenants of ... ...
vnto me in my behalfe, called the place Prouidence I ... ... it might be for a shelter for persons
for Conscience, then considering the condition of diuers of my ... ... Countreymen, I communi
cated my said purchase vnto my Louing frieindes John Throckmorton, William Arnold, William Harris, Stukeley
Westcott, John Greene senior, Thomas Olney senior, Richard Waterman and others, who then desired to
take Shelter here with me. ... In succession unto so many others as we should be receiued ... the ...
that were admitted our Townes fellowshipp and society of Commoning, And these of the said purchase: ... ...
And I Thomas Harris senior, William Wickenden, Robert Williams, Gregory Dexter, and others ... ...
Towne Bookes &c. And whereas by Gods mercifull Assistance I was the procurer, and more
purchase (not by monies nor payment, the Natiues being so shie) but ... ... other Aduantages
but it, but by that Language, Acquaintance, And fauour with the Natiues And fountains of all the Gouernment
which it pleased God to giue me, And also for the charges, ... Neighbourhood with them all, to my great charge ... ...
Louing that it pleased the great Sachims, And other Sachims the Natiues ... ...
Though his him by so some Louing friendes, that I should be some Louing consideration, I ... ...
.styling. ... ... thirty pound ...
... in joying Land And ... ... thirty Shillings and upward ... ...
first, about thirty pounds should be paid vnto me, ... thirty Shillings persons ...
They more admitte. ... this sum of thirty pounds, ... my selfe, Thirty Shillings I should haue
Townes, the place of succor for the ... ... in loue to my ... ...
Or payment, as full satisffaction for ... selfe, ... in the yeare one thousand six hundred ...
Thirty pound (so called) satisffaction, subscribed by ... ...
... Witnesses) signifyes Run their ... ...

...heirs, unto the whole number of the purchasers, with all my power, right, and title...
therein: Reserving only unto my selfe, one single share equal unto any of the rest of the number, of...
now Remaine, in the more Towarman way... as my hand and Seale confirme my former Resignation of...
the... of the Landes of... And binding my selfe, my heirs, my Executors, and Administrators...
... and Assignes, never to molest any of the said purchasers, Mizable heirs... or...
heirs unto the Society of purchasers as aforesaid. But that they, their Executors,
Administrators, and Assignes, shall at all tymes quietly, and peaceably, Enjoy the premises...
Every part thereof. And for further... the premises, bind my selfe, my heirs,
Executors, my Administrators, and Assignes never to lay any claime, nor Challenge any
Claime to be said to any of the Landes aforementioned, or unto any part, or parcell...
there of (more than unto my owne single share) by vertue, or presence of any...
Former Bargaine, Sale, or mortgage, what so ever; (or joynard... Either heirs, by, thou...
...said Roger Williams, or to any other person... unto...
In Witnesse whereof I have heerunto Sett my...
...June sixty one

                                                    Roger Williams.

Signed Sealed and
presented in the presence of
us
     Thomas Smith
     Joseph Carpenter

I Mary Williams, wife unto Roger Williams, doo Assent unto
the premises, witnesse my hand this twentieth of Decembor
in this present yeare one thousand six hund: and Sixty one

                                        the mark of M W Mary
                                                        Williams

Acknowledged and Subscribed
before and   William Hore Generall Assistant

Gratuetyes which I gave to the great Sachims, And other Sachims And Natives Round about us: And Lay ingaged for A Loving And pecable Neighbourhood with them all, to my great charge, And Travell; It was therefore Thought ffitt by some Loving ffreindes, that I should Recieve Some Loving consideration And gratuetye; And it was agreed between us, That Every person that should be Admitted into the ffelloship of injoying Land And desposing of the purchase should pay Thirtye Shillings unto a publique Stock; And ffirst about Thirtye pounds should be paid unto my selfe, by Thirtye Shillings A person, as They were Admitted: This Sum I Received, And in Love to my ffreindes, And with Respect to A Towne, And place of Succor for the destresed as aforesaid, I doe Acknowledg the Said Sum, And payment, as ffull Sattisffaction; And whereas in the yeare one Thousand six hundred Thirtye seauen (so called) I delivered the **deede** subscribed by the Two Aforesaid cheife Sachims (so much thereof as concerneth the afor-mentioned **Landes**) ffrom my selfe, And from my heires, unto the whole number of the purchasers, with all my powre, Right, And Title therein: Reserving only unto my selfe, one Single Share Equall unto any of the Rest of that number, I now Againe, in A more fformall way under my hand and Seale conffirme my fformer Resignation of that deede of the **Landes** aforsaid; And Bind my selfe, my heirs, my Exsecutors, my Administerators, And Assignes, never to molest any of the said persons Already Received, or hereafter to be Received into the Society of pur-chasers as aforsaid: But that they, theire heirs, Exsecutors, Administerators, And Assignes Shall at all tymes quietly, And pecably Injoy the premises, And Every part thereof; And I doe ffurther by these presentes, Bind my selfe, my heirs, my Exsecutors, my Administerators, And Assignes never to Lay any claime, nor cause any claime to be Laid to any of the **Landes** aformentioned, or unto any part, or percell thereof, (more than unto my owne Single Share) by Vertue, or pretence of any fformer Bargine, Sale, or Morgage, what So ever; (or jointers, Thirdes, or Intailes) made by me the said Roger Williams, or of any other person Either ffor, By, Through, or under me **Jn Wittnesse** thereof I have hereunto Sett my hand and Seall This Twentyeth day of December, in this presant yeare One Thousand Six hundred Sixty one

Memorandum the wordes: of the purchase was interlined before these presantes
was Sealed   ROGER WILLIAMS,

Signed, Sealed And Delivered
  in The presence of us
THOMAS SMITH
JOSEPH CARPENTER

> I MARY WILLIAMS, wife unto ROGER WILLIAMS, doe Assent unto
> the premises, Wittnes my hand this Twentieth of December
> in this presant yeare one Thousand Six hundred Sixty one
> Accknowledged And Subscribed
> before me William ffeild
> Gene^{rl} Assistant
> The marke of M W,   MARY
WILLIAMS."[1]

It would seem from this deed that the first twelve proprietors were admitted
into equal ownership of the lands with Roger Williams without being required to
furnish any equivalent for the value of the lands received, and that the thirty
pounds which were paid Roger Williams from the common fund created by the
payment of thirty shillings by each of the succeeding settlers was not paid as an
equivalent for the land, but was accepted by him as "a loving gratuity," and that
"all which he received was far less than what he had expended."

For the lands on the Pawtuxet river Mr. Williams received twelve-thirteenths
of twenty pounds from the twelve persons named in the deed of October 8, 1638.

The lands thus transferred by Roger Williams to his associates were divided
into two parts, which were known as "the grand purchase of Providence and the
Pautuxet purchase."

---

1. From the original in the office of the Recorder of Deeds, city of Providence.

The first inhabitants of Providence probably "settled in such places as were most convenient, and planted their corn on the old Indian fields as they could agree among themselves." As their numbers increased it became necessary to adopt a more systematic division of the lands, which resulted in the laying out of "the Towne Streete," now North and South Main streets, along the eastern shore of the river, and dividing the land eastward of the street into lots of five acres each, more or less, extending easterly to "the highway," now Hope street. These were the home lots or shares on which the dwellings of the proprietors were located.

The home lots at the northern portion of the town, near the place where Roger Williams and his companions landed, were laid out of a width of about one hundred and twenty-two feet. Between Dexter's lane, now Olney street, on the north, and the ancient "highway" which originally separated the home lots of William Carpenter and Robert Cole, now Meeting street, on the south, there are nineteen lots of an average width of about one hundred and twenty-two feet, and of an average area of about five and one-half acres, measured by the "eighteen foot pole."

The lots near the centre of the town being much longer, were considerably reduced in width. From Meeting street to Power's lane, now Power street, originally the dividing line between the lots of William Wickenden and Nicholas Power, there are twenty-one lots of an average width of about one hundred and seven feet, and an average area of a little more than five acres.

The lots near the southern extremity of the town being much shorter, were widened to one hundred and twenty feet, more or less. From Power street to the "highway" at the southern extremity of the town, now Wickenden street, there are twelve lots of an average width of about one hundred and twenty feet, and of an average area of about four and one-half acres each.

These divisions correspond very closely with the ancient landmarks which may yet be identified, as will appear from the following illustrations:

3

The distance from the south side of Meeting street to the north side of Thomas street, the southern boundary of the home lot of Thomas Angell, is about three hundred and twenty-one feet, comprising the three lots of Robert Cole, Thomas Olney, and Thomas Angell, allowing one hundred and seven feet for each.

From Thomas street to the northern line of the "What Cheer" building, which occupies the site of the home lot of Daniel Abbott, is about five hundred and thirty-five feet, or the five lots of one hundred and seven feet each originally laid out to Francis Weston, Richard Waterman, Ezekiel Holliman, Stukely West- cott, and William Reynolds.

From the south side of Power street to the northern boundary line of the ancient burial ground of the Tillinghast family, a well defined landmark, the dis- tance is nearly eight hundred and forty feet, and contains seven of the original lots of an average width of one hundred and twenty feet.

From the last mentioned boundary line to Wickenden street is about six hundred feet, comprising five lots of one hundred and twenty feet each.

These measurements are all approximate, and, as the variance would not exceed a very few feet, are sufficiently definite to serve the present purpose and to illustrate in a general way the plan herewith submitted. The areas are all estimated on the basis of the "eighteen foot pole." The records, however, show that some of the lots were of larger dimensions, and that others fell short of the required amount and were supplemented by additional grants of land.

In addition to the home lots, each proprietor had a six acre lot at a distance from his home lot, and also "stated common lots," either purchased or acquired by occasional dividends among themselves. Each settler's share, therefore, comprised the home lots, the upland for planting, the meadow, consisting of salt marsh or bog, whereon was cut the winter fodder for the cattle, and the woodland.

In a short time the number of inhabitants was considerably increased by accessions from the neighboring colonies, and a form of government was adopted which is embodied in the following agreement, there being no date appended to it in the original record:

"We whose names are hereunder desirous to inhabit in the town of Providence, do promise to subject ourselves in active and passive obedience, to all such orders or agreements as shall be made for public good of the body, in an orderly way, by the major consent of the present inhabitants, masters of families, incorporated together into a town fellowship, and others whom they shall admit unto them, only in civil things.

RICHARD SCOTT,	EDWARD COPE, ·
WILLIAM × RENOLDS	THOMAS × ANGELL,
CHAD BROWNE	THOMAS × HARRIS,
JOHN WARNER	FRANCIS × WEEKES,
JOHN × FEILD	BENEDICT ARNOLD
GEORGE RICKARD	JOSHUA WINSOR
	WILLIAM WICKENDEN."[1]

The compact of July 27, 1640, consisted of a report prepared by Robert Cole, Chad Brown, William Harris and John Warner, who had been "freely chosen" by their "loving friends and neighbors" to settle the "many differences" which had arisen among them. The report of these arbiters, containing proposals for a form of government, was signed by thirty-nine inhabitants of the town, and is noteworthy as having been the first departure from a pure democracy and the beginning of a town organization.

The following extracts from this compact are taken from "Staples' Annals of Providence," pp. 41–43:

Article second:

"Agreed. We have with one consent agreed, that for the disposing those lands that shall be disposed, belonging to this town of Providence, to be in the whole inhabitants by the choice of five men for general disposal, to be betrusted with disposal of lands and also of the town's stock and all general things, and not to receive in any in six days, as townsmen, but first to give the inhabitants

1. Deeds, &c., Trans., p. 1.

notice, to consider if any have just cause to show against the receiving of him, as you can apprehend, and to receive none but such as subscribe to this our determination. Also we agree, that if any of our neighbors do apprehend himself wronged by these or any of these five disposers, that at the general town meeting he may have a trial.

"Also, we agree for the town to choose beside the other five men, one to keep record of all things belonging to the town and lying in common.

" We agree, as formerly hath been the liberties of the town, so still to hold forth, liberty of conscience."

Article seven :

"Agreed, that the town by five men shall give every man a deed of all his lands lying within the bounds of the plantation to hold it by for after ages."

Article twelve :

" Agreed, that every man who hath not paid in his purchase money for his plantation shall make up his 10s. to be 30s. equal with the first purchasers, and for all that are received as townsmen hereafter, to pay the like sum of money to the town stock."

Roger Williams having effected a settlement at Providence, as we have seen, devoted the remaining years of his life to the welfare of the colony he had planted, and to the various duties, public and private, which devolved upon him as its father and founder.

In 1643 he sailed for England as an agent for the colonies of Providence, Rhode Island and Warwick, and obtained a charter of incorporation, signed by the Earl of Warwick, Governor and Admiral of the English Plantations, and by his Council. While there he published his " Key into the Language of America," which he had prepared during the voyage.

In 1651 he visited England a second time, in company with Rev. John Clarke, on matters of great public interest, and successfully accomplished the mission.

While in England he was the guest of Sir Henry Vane, at his residence in Lincolnshire, where he enjoyed the acquaintance of Cromwell, Milton and other leading spirits of the age. He returned to Providence in 1654, and on the 12th of September of that year he was chosen President of the colony, which office he held until May, 1658. He travelled much among the Indians and preached to them, securing the friendship of the chiefs and the warriors, which he retained to his latest days.

Roger Williams died sometime between January 16, 1682–3,[1] and April 25, 1683,[2] at about the age of 83 years, and "was buried with all the solemnity the colony was able to show." His remains were deposited in his own family burying-ground on his home lot, a short distance only from the place where his dwelling house stood.

The home lot of Roger Williams was located on the hillside easterly from the spring where he first landed, and immediately north of Bowen street. His house occupied very nearly the site of the present building on the northeast corner of North Main and Howland streets.

The western part of the home lot of Roger Williams, fronting on North Main street, is now in the possession of the heirs of Humphrey Almy, Matilda Metcalf and Harriet T. Richmond.

1. Roger Williams' signature is affixed to a document bearing this date, concerning the Pawtuxet lands.
2. On this date William Carpenter signed an instrument in which he states he was the last survivor of the thirteen original proprietors.

N.

MOOSHAUSICK RIVER

DEXTERS LANE

JOHN SMITH

MILL

SPRING

- GREGORY DEXTER
- MATTHEW WALLER.
- THOMAS PAINTOR.
- EDWARD MANTON.
- JOHN GREENE JR.
- BENEDICT ARNOLD.
- FRANCIS WICKES.
- THOMAS JAMES.
- JOHN GREENE SR.
- JOHN SMITH.
- WIDOW REEVE.
- JOSHUA VERIN.
- ROGER WILLIAMS.
- JOHN THROCKMORTON
- WILLIAM HARRIS.
- ALICE DANIELS.
- JOHN SWEET.
- WILLIAM CARPENTER.
- ROBERT COLE.
- THOMAS OLNEY.
- THOMAS ANGELL.
- FRANCIS WESTON.
- RICHARD WATERMAN.
- EZEKIEL HOLYMAN.
- STUKELY WESTCOTT.
- WILLIAM REYNOLDS.
- DANIEL ABBOTT.
- CHAD BROWN.
- JOHN WARNER.
- GEORGE RICKARD.
- RICHARD SCOTT.
- WILLIAM FIELD.
- JOHN FIELD.
- JOSHUA WINSOR.
- THOMAS HARRIS
- ADAM GOODWIN.
- WILLIAM BURROWS.
- WILLIAM MANN.
- WILLIAM WICKENDEN. POWERS LANE
- NICHOLAS POWER
- WIDOW JOAN TILER.
- WIDOW JANE SEARS.
- THOMAS HOPKINS.
- EDWARD HART.
- MATTHEW WESTON.
- JOHN LIPPITT.
- HUGH BEWITT.
- ROBERT WEST.
- WILLIAM HAWKINS.
- CHRISTOPHER UNTHA
- ROBERT WILLIAMS.

THE TOWNE STREETE

HIGHWAY

P

WAYBAUSSETT HILL

WAYBAUSSETT

NECK

PAUTUXETT ROAD

THE GREAT SALT RIVER

COW-PEN POINT

MILE END COVE

A.L. BODWELL, PHOTO ENG. PROV. R.I.

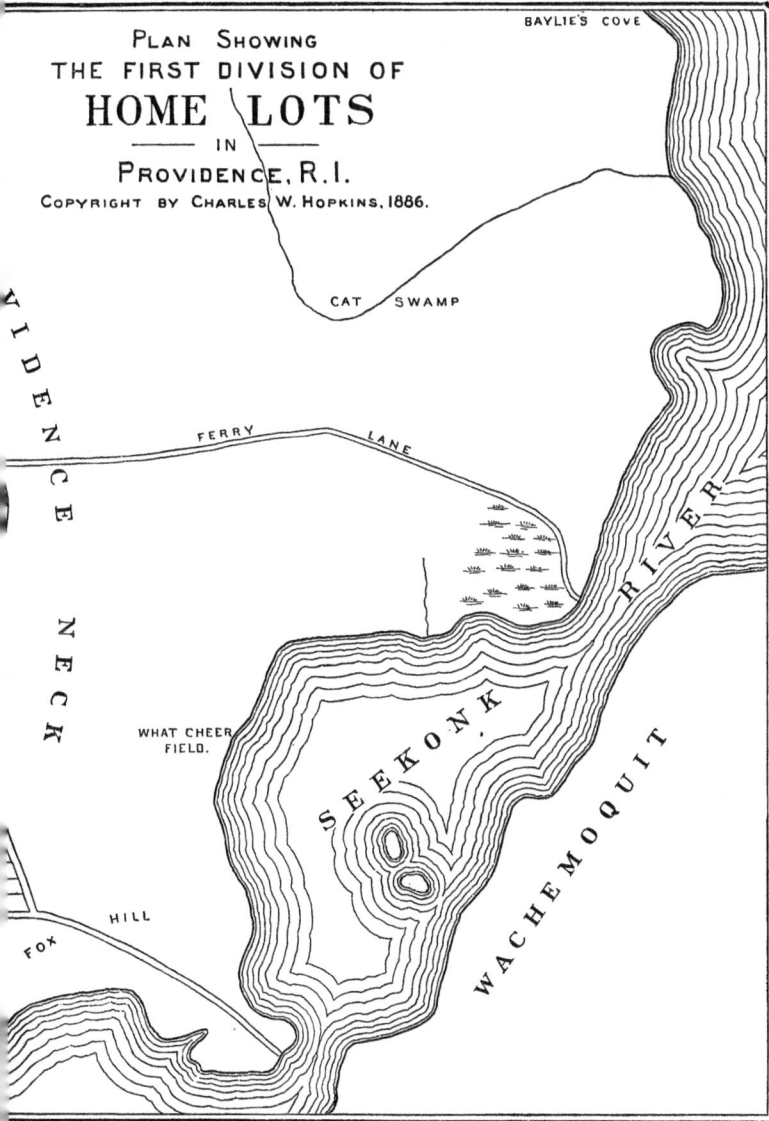

PLAN SHOWING
THE FIRST DIVISION OF
HOME LOTS
— IN —
PROVIDENCE, R.I.
COPYRIGHT BY CHARLES W. HOPKINS, 1886.

BAYLIE'S COVE

CAT SWAMP

FERRY LANE

SEEKONK RIVER

WACHEMOQUIT

WHAT CHEER FIELD.

HILL

FOX

NECK

VIDENCE

THE HOME LOTS.

THE following is a list of the homesteads of the early settlers of the Plantations founded by Roger Williams, commencing at Dexter's lane, now Olney
street, and extending to "Mile-End Cove," or Wickenden street. This
arrangement conforms more nearly to the order of settlement than that presented
in the original list, reproduced in the appendix.

It is believed that the accompanying notes, and extracts from the town records,
will be of interest and value not only to the numerous descendants so largely rep-
resented in the State of Rhode Island, but to the community at large, owing to the
fact that the present titles to these estates are founded upon the original records
here presented :

Gregory Dexter is said to have been born in London, where he followed
the business of printing. His imprint appears on the title-page of Roger
Williams' volume, "A Key into the Language of America," published in London
in 1643. He came to Providence about 1644, and was soon after received into the
Baptist Church, of which he afterwards (about 1650) became pastor. He was also
active in the civil affairs of the colony. His name is affixed to the compact of
July 27, 1640. He was elected to the office of Town Clerk for a number of years,
was chosen Commissioner to represent the town in the General Assembly and
served as President of Providence and Warwick in 1653-4. In 1654 he was

appointed with Roger Williams to write letters to Cromwell, Sir Henry Vane and others. Roger Williams speaks of him as "a man of education and of a noble calling and versed in militaries."

Morgan Edwards says of him: "Mr. Dexter by all accounts was not only a well-bred man, but remarkably pious. He was never observed to laugh, seldom to smile. So earnest was he in his ministry that he could hardly forbear preaching when he came into a house or met with a concourse of people out of doors."

His home lot was the most northerly of the fifty-two lots of the first division, and was bounded on the north by Dexter's lane, now Olney street. The home lot adjoining his on the south (Mathew Waller's) came into his possession as early as October 19, 1663. These two home lots of Gregory Dexter's are described as "a parcel of land . . . about ten acres & is two house lots . . . adjoining each to the other and bounding on the North part with a highway & on the East part with a highway, on the West part with the town street and on the South part with the land of Edward Manton."[1]

June 4, 1696:
"I, Gregory Dexter . . . do hereby freely give . . . unto my Grand son Peleg Dexter a house lot . . . containing five acres & part planted with apple trees & bounded on the west by the streete way & on the north by a highway, & on the East by a highway & on the south by a Lott that I gave to my grand daughter Isabel."[2]

The western part of Gregory Dexter's home lot is now in the possession of Mary R. Peckham, Emery H. Calder and Mrs. William H. Calder.

Mathew Waller signed the compact of 1640. His name also appears on the roll of freemen in Providence, 1655. His home lot became the property of Gregory Dexter, as appears by the record of the sale of the home lot (Thomas Painter's) "formerly Pardon Tillinghast's . . . 5 acres, bounded on the south

1. Trans., p. 336.   2. Deeds I, p. 231.

PLAN showing the approximate location of HOME LOTS of the
EARLY SETTLERS of PROVIDENCE, R.I.
COPYRIGHT BY C. W. HOPKINS.
1886.

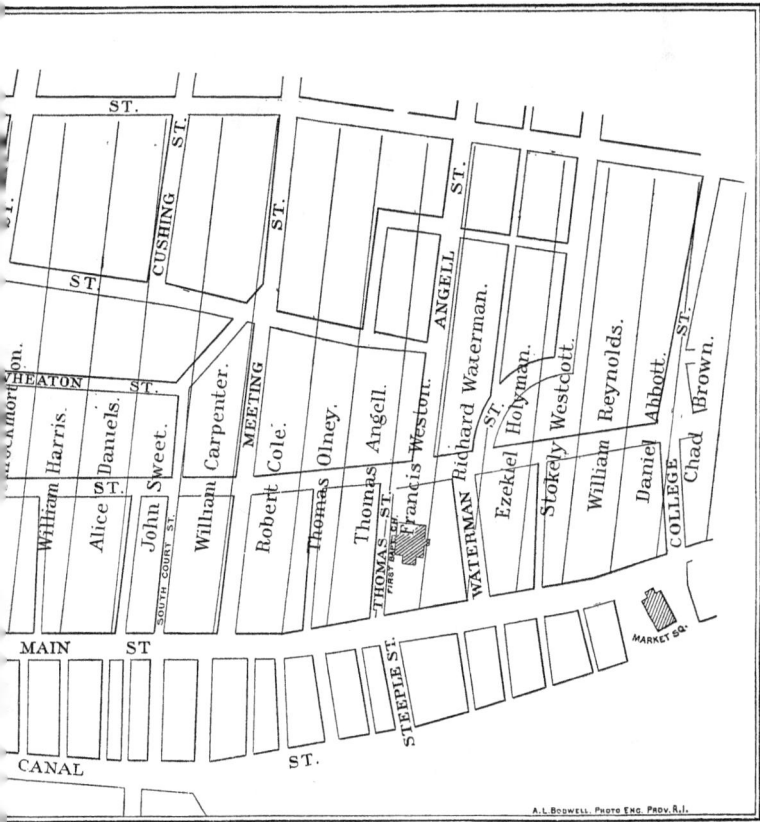

ST.

CUSHING ST.

ST.

ST.

ANGELL ST.

ST.

WHEATON

ST.

MEETING

ST.

WATERMAN

COLLEGE ST.

William Harris.

Alice Daniels.

John Sweet.

SOUTH COURT ST.

William Carpenter.

Robert Cole.

Thomas Olney.

Thomas Angell.

THOMAS ST.
FIRST BAPTIST CH.

Francis Weston.

Richard Waterman.

Ezekiel Holyman.

Stokely Westcott.

William Reynolds.

Daniel Abbott.

Chad Brown.

MAIN ST

CANAL

STEEPLE ST.

ST.

MARKET SQ.

A. L. BODWELL. PHOTO ENG. PROV. R. I.

by the home lot of Edward Manton, on the north by land " now in possession of Gregory Dexter."[1] This home lot of Mathew Waller's was given by Gregory Dexter to his grand-daughter Isabel.[2] The west end of this home lot is now owned by Morris Deming and Thomas D. Deming.

Thomas Painter had lot assigned him on the " Towne Streete." In 1655 his name appears on the roll of freemen of Newport. The home lot of Thomas Painter became the property of the town, and was assigned to Pardon Tillinghast, as appears from the following extract from the town records :

April 2, 1669 :

" I Henry Browne . . . have sold . . . unto Shadrac Manton . . . a house lot or home share of land with the dwelling house . . . which is upon the said lot . . . five acres more or less and is bounding on the south with the home lot of Edward Manton . . . on the north with the land now in the possession of Gregory Dexter . . . on the west or front with a fence . . . and is in breadth seven poles . . . I Henry Browne bought it of John ffenner . . . he . . . bought the said lot with the housing upon it of Pardon Tillinghast . . . the said lot Pardon Tillinghast received of the Town of Providence, being received into the Town according to their Order of a five and twenty acre right."[3]

February 26, 1668 :

" Voted and ordered, that Henry Browne his house and lot which he bought of John Fenner shall be made up full five Acres. . . . The said Henry Browne's lot is bounded on the South with the lot of Edward Manton and on the North with a lot belonging unto Gregory Dexter."[4]

A part of the west end of the home lot of Thomas Painter is now the property of Josiah W. Crooker.

Edward Manton received a home lot and signed the compact of 1640. January 27, 1667, Edward Manton's " house lot or home share whereon his house

1. Trans., p. 273. 2. Deeds I, p. 231. 3. Trans., p. 279. 4. Trans., p. 211.

4

standeth " is described as being bounded " on the north side with the lot of Henry Brown, south side bounding with a lot now belonging to John Whipple, Sen. . . . "[1]

The western part of the home lot of Edward Manton, fronting on Benefit street, is now the property of the City of Providence and is occupied by a school house.

John Greene, Jr., " Deputy Governor," was born in the year 1620. In 1642 his name appears as a witness to the purchase of Shawomet. He was elected Commissioner from Warwick from 1651 to 1659, when he was elected Assistant, and, with the exception of two years, was re-elected to this office for a period of twenty-six years. He also served as Attorney General for a number of years, and in 1654, and again in 1664 was appointed on a committee to revise the public laws. He served as Deputy Governor from 1690 to 1700, and died in Warwick, November 27, 1708.

The house in which he resided in Warwick is still standing in an excellent state of preservation, located on his homestead, now known as Spring Green Farm.

His home lot was in the possession of John Whipple, Sr., January 27, 1667. The western part of his home lot, fronting on Benefit street, is now owned by Henry J. Steere and Allen Greene.

Benedict Arnold, son of William, was born in England, December 21, 1615, and came to Providence in 1636. He received a grant of land and signed the first agreement, also the compact of 1640. He removed to Pawtuxet with his father, and in 1653 became a resident of Newport and was chosen Assistant. In 1658 he succeeded Mr. Williams as Governor, and continued in that office until 1660; also from 1662 to 1666, from 1669 to 1672, and from 1677 to 1678, in which last year he died. He was reputed to be the wealthiest man in the colony, and, excepting Roger Williams, was probably the most proficient in the language of the Indians.

The western part of his home lot, fronting on Benefit street, is now in the possession of Allen Greene and John Metcalf.

1. Trans., p. 202.

Francis Wickes was one of the five who accompanied Roger Williams on his first landing at Providence. He is supposed to have been a minor, as his name does not appear in the original deed from Williams. He received a home lot and signed the first agreement and the compact of 1640. His home lot became the property of John Whipple as early as November 23, 1663, as appears by the following extract from the town records: "On the north side with a home share of land which formerly belonged unto Francis Wickes, but now in the possession of me, John Whipple."[1]

The old "Whipple Tavern" was located on the "Towne Streete," within the limits of Francis Wickes' home lot, and occupied the site of 369 North Main street.

The western part of the home lot of Francis Wickes, fronting on Benefit street, is a part of the John Carter Brown and Ebenezer Kelley estates.

William Arnold, with his family, "Sett sayle ffrom Dartmouth in old England, the first of May, 1635," and arrived in New England, June 24th following. After residing a short time in Hingham, Mass., he removed with his family, in 1636, to Providence. He was one of the original proprietors of Providence, the second named in the initial deed, and signed the compact of 1640. In 1638 he removed to Pawtuxet, and in 1642, with others, placed himself under the jurisdiction of Massachusetts. In 1658 the General Court of Massachusetts, at their request, gave the Pawtuxet settlers permission to withdraw their allegiance from that colony.

"14st 2^{d} Mo. [April] 1641.

" The Town of Providence have appropriated to William Arnold his house share which containeth in length on the south part five score and twelve poles . . . and in breadth on the west part eight poles and on the east part eight poles . . . the poles being sixteen feet and one half . . . bounded with the home share of

---

1. Trans., p. 193.

Francis Wickes on the north part, and the house and lands that is now in the hands and occupation of Wm. Field on the south part, and the street on the west part, and a swamp on the east part. . . . And Also, another plat of ground lying without the north end of the town, upon part of which the said Wm. Arnold hath set up a Wolf trap."[1]

November 23, 1663:

" I, John Whipple of Providence have freely given unto my son John Whipple a house lot or home share of land which formerly belonged unto Wm. Arnold (now inhabitant of Pawtuxet,) with all the housing, fencing, fruit trees standing upon the said land . . . only excepting so much of the East part of the said lot which belongeth unto Thomas Olney of Prov. (Senior) which is about two acres. . . . The said share of land is in the Row of house lots in Providence . . . Bounding East with Thomas Olney . . . West with the street . . . On the north side with a home share of land which formerly belonged unto Francis Wickes . . . but now in the possession of me, John Whipple . . . on the south side with a home share of land formerly belonging unto Thomas James formerly inhabitant of Providence . . . but now in the possession of John Throckmorton. . . . The aforesaid lot or share of land containeth in breadth eight poles . . . sixteen feet and a half to the pole."[2]

John Whipple, Jr., having died December 15, 1700, his heirs, on the 22d day of April, 1701, in dividing the estate, gave the homestead lot, on which he lived, originally the home lot of William Arnold, to his son John Whipple, and also one-half of the adjoining home lot on the south (the home lot of Thomas James), purchased by John Whipple, Jr., of Alexander Bryant, it having formerly belonged to John Throckmorton. " The which half of said lot shall be that half of it all the length from the Towne Streete to the east end of said lot which is the northern half, and adjoineth to that lot whereon the said John Whipple's housing stands."[3]

---

1. Trans., p. 67.   2. Trans., p. 193.   3. Prov. Records, Old Book, No. II, p. 307.

"July 27, 1659, Quarter Day.

" This day John Whipple. Senr. is received into the Town a purchaser to have a purchase right of lands."[1]

Extract from the will of John Whipple, Sr., dated May 8, 1682 :

" I give unto my son Joseph my dwelling house & my three home lotts & ye Garden next ye River."

Date of the probate of the will, May 27, 1685.[2]

The western part of the home lot of William Arnold, fronting on Benefit street, is now in the possession of Mrs. Sarah J. S. Durfee, wife of Chief Justice Thomas Durfee.

Thomas James, an ordained minister, was the third named in the initial deed of Roger Williams to his twelve associates. He received a grant of land in Providence, June 10, [1637,] and was also one of the Pawtuxet purchasers. He sold his home lot to William Field, March 20, 1639, and it subsequently became the property of John Throckmorton, who was the owner November 23, 1663 ; Alexander Bryant and John Whipple, successively.

The western part of his home lot, fronting on Benefit street, is now in the possession of Mrs. Sarah J. S. Durfee, wife of Chief Justice Thomas Durfee.

John Greene, Sr., who was educated a surgeon, and had practiced in Salisbury, England, was the son of Richard and Mary (Hooker) Greene, of Bowridge Hill, Parish of Gillingham, Dorsetshire, England. He came from Hampton in the James of London, April 6, 1635, accompanied by his wife and five children. His first wife, Joan Tattersall, the mother of his six children, died at Conanicut in 1643, having fled to that island for safety at the time the Massachusetts troops

---

1. Trans., p. 105.   2. Wills II, p. 80.

made their unjustifiable and cruel assault upon the inhabitants of Warwick. His second wife was Alice Daniels, a widow, who had received a home lot in Providence. His third wife was Philip or Philippa, who survived him.

John Greene, Sr., was one of the thirteen original proprietors of Providence, the fifth named in the initial deed. October, 1642, he purchased of Myantonomi the tract of land Occupasnatuxet, now known as the Spring Green Farm, in Warwick. January 12, 1642–3, he, with others, purchased Shawomet, or Warwick, of Myantonomi. August 8, 1643, he was a member of the first town council of Warwick, and in 1652 and 1653 served as General Recorder. He was prominent in the colonial affairs of Providence and Warwick, and the loss of his professional services upon his removal to Warwick must have been keenly felt by the people of Providence. He was the ancestor of General Nathanael Greene and of others who have borne a prominent part in the history of the State and nation.

John Greene, Sr., "On the 25 September, 1644 sold his interest in the Providence purchase to his son John. At that time he was residing at Occupassua-tuxet, in Warwick. The General Court of Massachusetts, in October, 1658, granted him leave to visit his friends there, for one month, 'sometime in the next summer, he behaving himself peaceably and inoffensively.' . . . John Greene was prevented by death from availing himself of this liberty. He died in the winter of 1658. . . ."[1]

The western part of the home lot of John Greene, Senior, fronting on North Main street, is now in the possession of Mrs. Raymond G. Hodges, Mary K. Newell and Mrs. George B. Calder.

John Smith (the miller) came to Providence in 1636. Roger Williams, before the Court of Commissioners, said, "I consented to John Smith, miller at Dorchester, (banished also) to go with me."

1. Collections of the Rhode Island Historical Society, Vol. 2, p. 89.

" 1st of the 1st mo. [March] 1646 so called.

" It was agreed that John Smith have the valley wherein his house stands in case he set up a mill." The offer was accepted and the mill built. He died between 1647 and the 10th of May, 1649.

April 30, 1713, the home lot originally assigned to John Smith, miller, was in the possession of the heirs of Major John Dexter, deceased.[1] The present owners of the western part of the home lot of the above John Smith are Sophia Daniels, George J. Thurber, Newton C. Dana, and Mary T. Rivers.

Widow Reeve had been a member of the church at Salem, and upon removing to Providence received a home lot in the first division of lands. This home lot came into the possession of Richard Scott, and was by John Scott sold to Charles Dier,[2] who sold it April 30, 1713, together with the home lot adjoining it on the south (the home lot of Joshua Verin), to Nathaniel Brown.[3] The western part of this lot was occupied by " The Church of England," or " King's Church," as it was called, as early as 1722, it having been transferred to the church by deeds of gift from Nathaniel Brown, dated September 18 and 19, 1722.[4] (See Joshua Verin.) The origin of this church is due in a great measure " to the persevering piety and untiring zeal of Gabriel Bernon," one of its first Wardens, who is buried beneath the church, and in whose memory a mural tablet has been erected. This edifice received the name of St. John's Church by act of incorporation 1794. The corner-stone of the present church, occupying the same site, was laid Tuesday, June 5, 1810, the old church having been demolished in April of that year.

Joshua Verin was one of the five who accompanied Roger Williams on his first visit to Providence, and received an early grant of land.

May 21st, second year of the Plantation, it was ordered that " Joshua Verin, for breach of covenant in restraining liberty of conscience, shall be withheld the liberty

---

1. Deeds II, p. 300.   2. Deeds II, p. 347.   3. Deeds II, p. 300.   4. Deeds V, p. 190-192.

of voting, till he declare the contrary." He had restrained his wife from attending religious meetings as often as she desired. He removed to Salem, and November 21, 1650, sent a letter to the town of Providence claiming a right to land as one of the six original proprietors. An answer was returned that justice would be done him should he come into court and prove his right.

January 28, 1674–5 :

"Laid out unto John Whipple Jun. Atturney unto Joshua Verin in ye right of the said Verin now of Barbadoes in Saint James parrish, formerly an inhabitant of this town—four score and fourteen acres of land being part of his purchase right in ye first division, (the other part being his house lot and one share of salt meadow which he sold unto Mr. Richard Scott of said Towne)."[1]

"Samuell Whipple of Providence being of full age testifyeth & saith that his Brother John Whipple he Vnderstood had A Letter of Aturney from Joshua Verin to Challinge his whole wright & he sd Whipple being Consairned About it this deponant asked Richard Scott of sd towne wether he had bought his home lote & his share of salt medow & furder this deponant saith that said Scott said that he thought he had bought all sd Verin's Right in providence but upon search of his deed he found he had bought no more than his hows Lote and his medow and claimed no more than his deed mentioned.

taken or ingaged this 28th of May 1705.

JOSEPH WILLIAMS

Assistant."[2]

April 30, 1713:

"Charles Dire of Providence . . . for and in consideration of the sum of Three Hundred Pounds of Current Money sold unto Nathaniel Brown of Rehoboth, Shipwright . . . certain lands, meadows & Privileges . . . in Providence aforesaid the which formerly belonged to Richard Scott of said Providence, deceased as namely two Home lots lieing in the Towne being in Estimation

---

1. Deeds I, p. 59.

2. The author is indebted to Mr. Fred. A. Arnold, of Providence, for this transcript from the Foster Papers, No. 13, p. 14, and for other similar favors.

thirteen acres & are bounded on the south with the lot belonging to the Heirs of Daniel Williams (deceased) & on the north with land belonging to the Heirs of Major John Dexter (deceased) & on the East with a Highway & on the west with the Towne street . . . and also all other lands of what sort soever either devided or undevided which formally belonged to ye said deceased Richard Scott of sd Providence; that is to say, all those that I bought of Mr. John Scot of Newport in the Colony aforesaid and was not before disposed of."[1]

The two home lots sold as above were originally the home lots of Widow Reeve and Joshua Verin, and are believed to have been occupied at a later period as the residence of Richard Scott, and also of William and Mary Dyer. It was from her home at this place that Mary Dyer is said to have gone forth to suffer martyrdom at Boston as a preacher of the Society of Friends.

The western front of the home lot of Joshua Verin is now in the possession of the heirs of Joseph Fletcher and Mrs. James Snow, Jr.

Roger Williams. (See pages 1 to 17.)

John Throckmorton sailed from Bristol, England, December 1, 1630, in company with Roger Williams. "He had been an officer of an English corporation and had some acquaintance with law." He and his wife were members of the church at Salem, and later became original members of the church at Providence. He was the sixth named in the initial deed. He signed the compact of 1640, and was appointed Deputy for the years 1664, '65 and '66. In 1667 he was exonerated from the charge made against him and others by William Harris. He became one of the earliest of Fox's converts.

The home lot of John Throckmorton was in the possession of Samuel Right, January 4, 1704–5.[2]

The western front of his home lot is now in the possession of William Ames, trustee, and Anna O. Greene.

---

1. Deeds II, p. 300.   2. Deeds III, p. 53.

William Harris "arrived at Salem in 1635." He removed to Providence with Williams and became one of the original proprietors, the seventh named in the initial deed, and was one of the four proprietors of the Pawtuxet purchase who placed themselves under the jurisdiction of Massachusetts. He was one of the four arbiters appointed to prepare a plan of government in 1640, one of the two town magistrates of Providence in 1655, and a Commissioner to represent the town of Providence in 1657-58-62-63. "Harris and Olney were the first surveyors of Providence." "Harris had probably been an attorney or attorney's clerk."

In 1667 he was deposed from his office of Assistant and a fine of £50 was imposed by the General Assembly for his procuring the Assembly to be called without sufficient cause. The fine was subsequently remitted.

He was bitterly opposed to Roger Williams in matters pertaining to the proprietorship of the lands.

"On the 24th of January, 1679, he sailed for England on board of the ship Unity of Boston, William Condy, master, as agent of the Pawtuxet purchasers. In the course of this voyage he was taken by a Barbary corsair and carried to Algiers, where he remained in captivity more than a year. He was redeemed at the cost of about \$1200, travelled through Spain and France, and arrived in London in 1680, and died the third day after his arrival at the house of his friend, John Sailes. He executed his will at Newport before he sailed for England. That is dated Dec. 4, 1678. . . . It was afterwards proved at Providence, Feb. 20, 1682."[1]

The home lot of William Harris became the property of Daniel Brown, who sold it to Daniel Williams, as appears by the following extract from the town records :

January 4, 1704-5 :

" I, Daniel Brown . . . have sold . . . one house lot in Providence Joyning to the house lot of Samuel Right now in possession on the north and on the south to a Lott that was formerly Valentine Whitmans . . . to Daniel Williams."[2]

---

1. Col. R. I. Hist. Soc'y, Vol. 2, p. 113.   2. Deeds III, p. 53.

The western front of the home lot of William Harris is now owned by Albert D. Yeomans, Martha A. Yeomans, and Albert L. Calder.

Alice Daniels received a grant of land the second year of the Plantation. She married John Greene, Sr., and her home lot was sold to Valentine Whitman, as appears from the following extract from the town records:

"Nov. 27, 1657. . . . John Greene Sen. sold to Valentine Whitman a house lot lying between the lot of William Harris on the north and Edward Manton on the south."[1]

March 6, 1685:

"I, Valentine Whitman . . . for a valuable sum of silver money in hand . . . paid by Daniel Williams . . . have sold . . . my House and House Lott . . . bounding on the northern side with a home share of Land now in the possession of the said Daniel Williams the which belonged unto William Harris of said Providence, now deceased and on the southern side with a home share of land now in the possession of Shadrac Manton . . . containing by estimation about seven acres."[2]

The western front of the home lot of Alice Daniels is now in the possession of Thomas Furlong.

John Sweet received a home lot in the first division of lands at Providence. He removed to Warwick, and was chosen Commissioner in 1653.

His home lot became the property of Edward Manton, as appears from the following extract from the town record:

"Nov. 27, 1657:

"John Greene Sen. sold to Valentine Whitman a house lot lying between the lot of Wm. Harris on the north and Edward Manton on the south."[3]

This home lot was owned by Shadrac Manton, March 6, 1685. The western part of this lot is now occupied by the State House.

1. Trans., p. 80.   2. Deeds IX, p. 365.   3. Trans., p. 80.

William Carpenter, son of Richard, of Amesbury, Wiltshire, England, came to Providence in 1636. He was one of the original proprietors, the eighth named in the initial deed, and received a home lot and signed the compact of 1640.

In 1642 he, with his father-in-law, William Arnold, and two others, subjected himself to the jurisdiction of Massachusetts, but was released in 1658 at his own request. He served as Commissioner from Providence from 1658 to 1663, and as Assistant for the years 1665, '66, '67, '69, '71. He was one of the original members of the church at Providence.

The home lot of William Carpenter is described as being the lot that " Lieth adjoining on the north side of the highway [now Meeting street] which Leadeth from the Towne street into the neck," and was given by Thomas Olney, Jr., to his son William by will dated February 20, 1721–2. (See Thomas Olney.)

The western part of the home lot of William Carpenter is now the property of the Friends' Society, having been purchased in 1727, as appears by the following record of a meeting of the Society and the accompanying notes :

" 9th Month (November) 1724 :

" Whereas it is concluded by this meeting, a house shall be built in Providence town, and there being a frame offered to us, it is concluded by this meeting that if Edward Smith and Thomas Arnold approve of the frame, that the money be paid to Daniel Abbott, as quick as can be, with convenience.

" The house was probably built soon after this, and is a part of the meeting house now standing between South Court street and Meeting street. The deed of the lot was made in the beginning of the year 1727, and describes it as then having on it a meeting house. An addition was subsequently made to it in the years 1784–5."[1]

Robert Cole " came to this country, probably, with the first settlers of Massachusetts. His name is among those who desired to be made freemen, in October, 1630, and he was admitted a freeman on the 18th of May following."[2]

1. Staples' Annals of Prov., pp. 428–430.   2. Col. R. I. Hist. Soc'y, Vol. II, p. 50.

He received a grant of land in Providence, June 10, [1637,] was the fourth named in the initial deed, and was one of the four arbiters who reported a form of government in 1640. He was one of the four original proprietors of Pawtuxet who subjected themselves to Massachusetts. He became one of the inhabitants of Shawomet, and "died before November, 1655, as appears from a deed of that date, made by John Coles to Mary Coles, widow of Robert Coles, of his interest in his father's estate."[1]

The 3d of the 11th month [Jan.], 1652:

"Robert Coles sold unto Richard Pray and Mary the wife of the said Richard Pray his house and house lot lying betwixt the house lot of Thomas Olney on the south and the highway whereon the Pound standeth on the north."[2]

The eastern end of this home lot was given by Thomas Olney, son of Thomas, Sr., to his son William in his will, bearing date February 20, 1720–1, he having purchased it of William Pray. (See Thomas Olney.)

The western part of the home lot of Robert Cole is now in the possession of Samuel M. Noyes, William V. Wallace, Mrs. Elizabeth B. Updike, Mrs. Charles H. Henshaw, Mrs. Reginald A. Howe, and A. B. Adams.

Thomas Olney came from Hertford, England, in 1635, with his wife Mary (Small) and two children. He was a member of the church at Salem, and became one of the original members of the church at Providence. "The records of the town show that Thomas Olney, senior, came to Providence about 1638. He was there baptized, with his wife, about 1639. They had a son Thomas, who came with them, a minor, and who was afterwards town clerk for many years. He is probably the person referred to [as pastor] in the church records."[3] Thomas Olney, Jr., was born in Hertford, England, in 1631.

Thomas Olney, Sr., was the ninth named in the initial deed from Roger Williams to his twelve associates, and received a home lot and signed the compact of 1640. He was the first town treasurer of Providence, one of the first sur-

1. Col. R. I. Hist. Soc'y, Vol. II, p. 50.   2. Trans., p. 78.   3. Annals of Prov., p. 411.

veyors.; also one of the first Commissioners, and was appointed to the office of Assistant for a number of years. By will dated March 21, 1679, he gave his house lot and home share to his son, Thomas Olney,[1] who gave it to his son William, as appears by the following extract from the will of Thomas Olney, Jr.:

" I, Thomas Olney Sen. [son of Thomas, Sen] . . . Give and bequeathe unto my son William Olney my two home Lotts situate Lieing 'and being in said Providence Towne, one of the which Lotts was my father Thomas Olney his homestead and Lieth adjoining on the north side of that which was the homestead Lott of Thomas Angell, deceased, and on the south side of that which was the homestead Lott of Robert Cole, deceased, the other of said Lotts Lieth adjoining on the north side of the highway which Leadeth from the Towne streete into the neck, being that Lott which was originally the Lott of William Carpenter, deceased, Each Lott containing of about six acres and half or seven acres of land, and also the eastern end of that Lott of Land which was originally the house Lott or homestead Lott of the aforesaid Robert Cole and since the homestead of Richard Pray, deceased, the which I purchased of William Pray."

Date of will, February 20, 1721-2.[2] The above Thomas Olney died June 11, 1722. The western part of Thomas Olney's home lot is now owned by the City of Providence.

Thomas Angell "came originally from London" and was one of the number who accompanied Roger Williams at his first landing at Providence. He is mentioned as "a young lad living in the family of Roger Williams," and received a grant of land, and signed the first agreement and the compact of 1640. He acquired possession of the home lot adjoining his own on the south, originally Francis Weston's, as appears by the following:

"Where is now Thomas street was the original site of the Angells. They added to their original home lot the square immediately to the south of it, part of which until 1774 was an orchard."[3]

1. Wills I, p. 43.   2. Wills II, p. 126.   3. Planting and Growth of Providence, p. 37.

Extract from Thomas Angell's will: " I do give and bequeathe unto my son James Angell my dwelling house . . . and my house lot or share of land whereon the said house standeth, together with my other house lot or home share of land to it adjoining."[1] Date of will, May 23, 1685. Date of probate of will, September 18, 1694.

" I James Angell of Providence . . . Quitclaim unto my brother John Angell . . . two home lots which formerly belonged to my honored father James Angell, deceased . . . his homestead, the which two lotts of land bound-eth as follows . . . on the north with the land of Mr. Thomas Olney and on the south with the land of Mr. Nathaniel Waterman and on the East with a high-way and on the west with the Towne streete, excepting only a small piece I Reserve at the North West Corner adjoining to the town streete, that is to say to extend from the said Thomas Olney's land southward twelve yards and from the Towne Streete Eastward twenty yards."[2] April 4, 1711.

The western front of the home lot of Thomas Angell is now owned by Eliza F. Man, Anna H. Man, and the heirs of William Goddard.

Francis Weston was admitted a freeman of Massachusetts in November, 1633. He was one of the deputies from Salem to the General Court in 1634, and after his removal to Providence was the tenth named in the initial deed of Williams to his associates. He joined in the purchase of Warwick, and became one of the victims of the raid by the Massachusetts soldiery upon that unhappy colony, having " through cold and hardship in prison, fell into a consumption, and in a short time after [before June 4, 1645,] died of it."[3]

Thus perished as a martyr, sentenced for " heresy," "to be set on work and to wear such bolts and irons as may hinder his escape "[4] from the prison at Dorchester, the original owner of the home lot in Providence whereon now stands the first Baptist church in America, of which he was one of the original members.

1. Wills I, p. 205.   3. Col. R. I. Hist. Soc'y, Vol. II, pp. 90 and 102.
2. Deeds II, p. 617.   4. Ibid, p. 277.

The home lot of Francis Weston became the property· of Thomas Angell, (see Thomas Angell,) and was by him given to his son James by will, dated May 23, 1685, and by James, son of the above James, was transferred by deed, April 4, 1711, to his brother John, who sold the portion of it now occupied by the First Baptist Church to William Russell, in 1774, by whom it was in the same year transferred to the First Baptist Society. "This church was opened for public worship for the first time on the 28th day of May, 1775, though it was not completed until some months after this." The first twelve members of this church were Roger Williams, Ezekiel Holliman, William Arnold, William Harris, Stukely Westcott, John Greene, Richard Waterman, Thomas James, Robert Cole, William Carpenter, Francis Weston, and Thomas Olney.[1]

Richard Waterman, according to Felt's "Annals of Salem," arrived at Salem on the 16th day of June, 1629. "On the 12th March, 1638, he was licensed by the General Court of Massachusetts to remove out of that jurisdiction, provided he removed his family before the next General Court. Francis Weston, Stukely Westcott, Richard Carder, Thomas Olney and others were also included in the same sentence."[2] He removed from Salem after Williams's banishment and settled with him at Providence, and was the eleventh named in the initial deed. He served as member of the Town Council, 1651, and was a Commissioner for the years 1650–2–5–6. He acquired possession of the home lot of Ezekiel Holliman, the lot next south of his own, and was also one of the purchasers of Shawomet. "He did not remove to Shawomet, but resided at Providence and Newport till his death, which was in the month of October, 1673." He was buried on that portion of his estate which was originally the home lot of Ezekiel Holliman. A granite monument marks the spot.

The western front of the home lot of Richard Waterman is now owned by the Charitable Baptist Society, and is the southern part of the lot now occupied by the First Baptist Church.

---

1. Benedict's History of the Baptists, Vol. I, p. 473.   2. Col. R. I. Hist. Soc'y, Vol. II, p. 88.

Ezekiel Holliman is said to have been born at Tring, Hertford county, England. He came to this country about 1634, and in 1637 was a resident of Salem. He removed to Providence, and was the twelfth and last named in the initial deed.

In 1638–9, Roger Williams becoming dissatisfied with his early baptism, it was decided that Ezekiel Holliman, "a man of gifts and piety," should be appointed to administer the ordinance by immersion, which being done, Mr. Williams in return baptized Mr. Holliman and ten others. This was the origin of the present First Baptist Church of Providence. This church was ministered to by Roger Williams, Ezekiel Holliman being his assistant.

Soon after the settlement of the church, about 1642, Holliman removed to Warwick, where he filled offices of trust. He was appointed Deputy to the General Court, and also one of the Commissioners for reuniting Providence, Portsmouth, Newport and Warwick into one corporate body.

Hugh Bewit became the owner of the home lot of Ezekiel Holliman, as appears from the following extract from the town records :

" 27th 11th mo. [Jan.] 1650:

" Hugh Bewit sold unto Richard Waterman his house & house lot lying next to the house lot of the said Richard Waterman whereon he now dwells and on the South Side lyeth Stukely Westcott's house lot."[1]

The western part of Ezekiel Holliman's home lot is now included in the Waterman estate.

Stukely Westcott and wife were members of the church at Salem. They removed to Providence in April, 1638, were baptized by Roger Williams, and became original members of the Baptist Church.

His name is the first mentioned in the initial deed from Roger Williams to his twelve associates, the original proprietors. He received a home lot, signed the com-

---

1. Trans., p. 125.

pact of 1640, and a few years later removed to Warwick, where he was appointed Commissioner to represent the town, which office he held for a number of years, and died in 1677 at an advanced age.

" 12th 3^d month [May] 1652.

"Stukely Westcott sold to Samuel Bennett his house and house lot lying betwixt Richard Waterman & Robert Williams house lot with Orchard and all other appurtenances thereto belonging."[1]   Also other lands.

The present owners of the western front of the home lot of Stukely Westcott are Thomas Breck, James T. Rhodes estate, Hiram B. Aylesworth, Eliza B. Patten, and Newton Dexter.

William Reynolds received a grant of land in the second year of the Plantation. He signed the first agreement, also the compact of 1640.

February 8, 1664–5, Robert Williams, of Newport, schoolmaster, sold to John Scott, of Providence, " his dwelling house in Providence with ye housing, home share and orchard as I bought them of Wm. Reynolds."[2]

The present owners of western part of William Reynolds' home lot are Eliza B. Patten, and Newton Dexter.

Daniel Abbott received a home lot. He " stayed and went not away " during King Philip's war. At the close of the war he was appointed town clerk, and the records which had been preserved were " handed over to him." December 22, 1679, he petitioned the town " that they agree lovingly together for the building them a town house to keep their meetings in," which appears not to have been favorably received.

" Providence, 27th 8th mo. [Oct.] 1644 (so called)."

Robert Morris sold to Robert Williams " ye house and ground which lies between William Reynolds and Chad Brown, so much as lies between the fence."[3]

1. Trans., p. 77.   2. Deeds I, p. 4.   3. Deeds I, p. 10.

Plan showing the approxima
location of HOME LOTS
EARLY SETTLERS ở PROVI
COPYRIGHT BY C
18

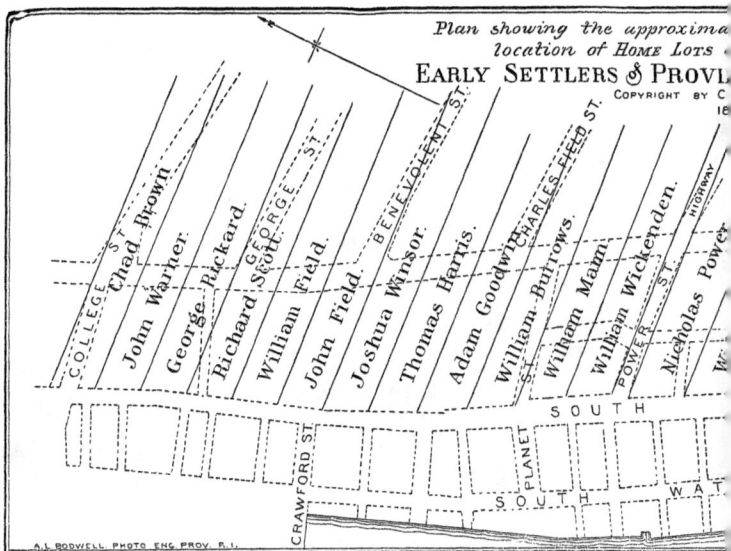

COLLEGE ST.
Chad. Brown
John Warner.
George Rickard.
Richard Scott.
GEORGE ST.
William Field.
John Field.
Joshua Winsor.
BENEVOLENT ST.
Thomas Harris.
Adam Goodwin
CHARLES FIELD ST.
William Burrows.
William Mann.
William Wickenden.
POWER ST.
HIGHWAY
Nicholas Power
CRAWFORD ST.
SOUTH
PLANET
SOUTH
SOUTH
WAT

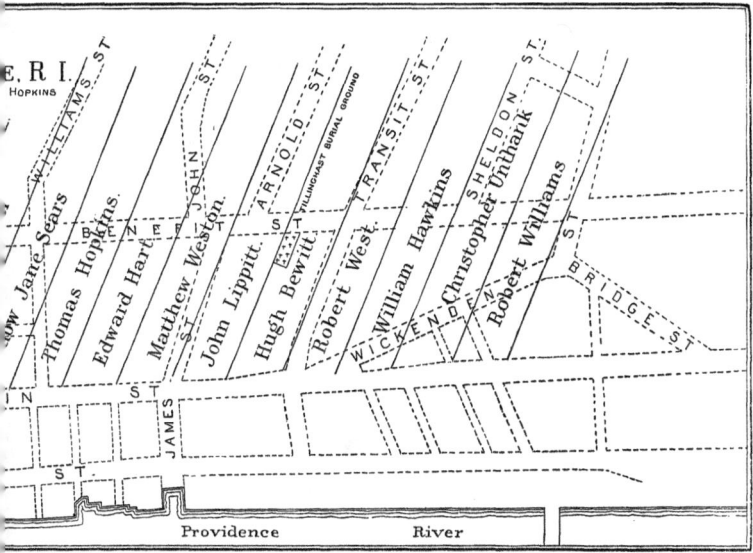

E. R. I.
HOPKINS

WILLIAMS ST.

ST.

ARNOLD ST.

TILLINGHAST BURIAL GROUND

TRANSIT ST.

SHELDON ST.

Jane Sears

Thomas Hopkins

Edward Hart

JEFFERSON ST.

JOHN ST.

Matthew Weston.

John Lippitt.

Hugh Bewitt.

Robert West.

William Hawkins

WICKENDEN ST.

Christopher Unthank

Robert Williams

ST.

BRIDGE ST.

IN

ST.

JAMES

ST.

Providence   River

October 1, 1665, Robert Williams sold to " Daniel Abbott (who formerly was my servant) . . . a house lot or home share of land . . . 5 acres, more or less, . . . in ye row of house lots, . . . bounded east by common, west by town street or common highway, north by land of John Scott, south by home lot or home share formerly belonging to Chad Brown dec'd—now Thomas Bakers . . . Ye said house lot or home share originally belonged to Daniel Abbott, Sen. father of the above said Daniel Abbott and was sold by Daniel Abbott, Sen. to Robert Morris and by Morris to me said Robert Williams."[1]

The western front of this home lot is now owned by the What Cheer Corporation.

Chad Brown, " the first elder " of the Baptist Church in Providence, was born in England about the year 1600. It is supposed that he came to America in the ship Martin, July, 1638. He came to Providence soon after its settlement, was a signer of the first agreement, and one of the number appointed to draw up the compact of 1640. He was formally ordained pastor of the church in Providence in 1642, and performed the duties of the office until his death, which occurred not far from 1663. He was one of the early surveyors of Providence.

" Roger Williams, in his plea before the Court of the New England Colonies, in Providence, in the year 1677, gives the following brief but comprehensive view of Mr. Brown's character and personal influence :

" The truth is, Chad Browne, that wise and godly soul (now with God) with myself, brought the remaining aftercomers and the first twelve to a oneness by arbitration."[2]

" It appears that the committee which formed the original list of lots, and probably the " Towne Streete," on which they lay, consisted of Chad Brown, John Throckmorton, and Gregory Dexter."[3]

1. Deeds I, p. 10.
2. James Manning and the Early History of Brown University, by Reuben Aldridge Guild, p. 145.
3. Dorr's Planting and Growth of Providence, p. 18.

December 31, 1672:

"I John Brown of Providence . . . have freely given . . . unto my brother James Browne of Newport . . . a House Lott, or Home share . . . sd parcell of Land formerly belonged unto my father Chadd Browne (now deceased) he being possessed with ye same from ye aforesaid Towne of Providence . . . It being his House Lott or home Share & containing in quantity about five acres, (more or less,) It bounding on ye northern side with a home share of land formerly belonging unto Daniel Abbott of ye said Towne of Providence (deceased) but now in ye possession of Daniel Abbott his son, on ye Southerne side with a home share of Land formerly belonging unto George Rickards (Deceased) but now in ye possession of Mrs. Deborah ffeild, on ye Eastern End with ye common on ye western end with a highway or Towne Strett . . . The sd share of Land became my Right by Recession from my mother Elizabeth my father's wife according as my sd father Chad Browne by his will disposed ye same . . . Reserving only to myself my heirs & assigns Twenty foott square of ye sd Land with ye orchard where my sd father & mother is buried, with free egress from ye sd place."[1]

December 31, 1672, James Brown sold the above described home lot to Daniel Abbott.[2]

In 1723 the Congregational Society erected their first house of worship in Providence at the corner of College and Benefit streets, on land originally the home lot of Chad Brown. The Society sold this house to the town in 1794 and built a more spacious and elegant one at the corner of Benevolent and Benefit streets, which was dedicated August 16, 1795. This house was ornamented with two spires, and was a beautiful copy of one of the most beautiful houses of worship in Boston. It was destroyed by fire on the morning of the 14th of June, 1814. The church now occupying the same site was dedicated on the 31st of October, 1816.[3]

Brown University is located upon the home lot of Chad Brown, the ancestor of Nicholas Brown, its most munificent benefactor. The University grounds also

---

1. Deeds I, p. 11.   2. Deeds I, p. 12.   3. Staples' Annals Prov., pp. 438–439.

include portions of the home lots of Daniel Abbott and William Reynolds on the north, and John Warner and George Rickard on the south.

The present owners of the western front of the home lot of Chad Brown are William M. Bailey, trustee for Mrs. A. G. Van Zandt, and Marshall Woods and wife.

John Warner, a "citizen and freeman of London," signed the first agreement, and was one of the four arbiters who reported a form of government in 1640. January 12, 1642-3, he joined with ten others in the purchase of Shawomet, or Warwick, "for one hundreth and ffortie 4 ffatham of wamppampeague." " The first records of Warwick appear to be in his handwriting. He was Town Clerk, member of the Town Council, Deputy and Assistant for the town of Warwick, between the years 1647 and 1652. He was also Clerk or Secretary of the General Court of the Colony of Providence Plantations in 1648."[1] On the 24th of April, 1652, at a town meeting in Warwick, John Warner, for grave misdemeanors, was degraded from holding any office in the town until he give the town satisfaction.

December 16, 1663, George Kenrick of Newport sold to William Field of Providence a lot of land "formerly the home share of John Warner . . . about 3 1-2 acres. . . . Bounded east with a parcel of land now in the possession of Thomas Baker of Newport, the which parcel of land was formerly part of the above named lot . . . west with the town street or highway, on the north side with the home share of land of Chadd Brown deceased, but now in the possession of the aforesaid Thomas Baker his successor, and on the south side with the land of the aforesaid William Field. . . . The said John Warner also building the said house upon the aforesaid land and afterward did by sale pass away the said house and land unto the above named Wm. Field who transferred it to George Rickard also formerly an inhabitant of the said town of Providence the said house and land being after the decease of the aforesaid Geo. Rickard by will disposed of unto me the said Geo. Kendrick."[2]

Present owners of the western front of the home lot of John Warner: John Carter Brown estate, Hope B. Russell, and Amasa S. Westcott.

1. Col. of R. I. Hist. Soc'y, Vol. II, p. 55.   2. Trans., p. 35.

George Rickard signed the first agreement and received a home lot. He purchased of William Field the house and home lot originally John Warner's, and died previous to December 16, 1663.

The home lot of George Rickard, after his decease, became the property of Mrs. Deborah Field, as appears by the following from the town records:

December 31, 1672:

" I, John Brown, . . . have freely given . . . unto my brother James Brown . . . a House Lott or home share . . . sd parcel of land formerly belonged to my father, Chadd Browne (now deceased) . . . bounding on ye northern side with a home share of land formerly belonging unto Daniel Abbott . . . (deceased) . . . on ye Southern side with a home share of land formerly belonging unto George Rickards (Deceased) but now in ye possession of Mrs. Deborah ffeild."[1]

John Brown, son of Chad Brown, on the 3d of December, 1672, purchased the eastern part of George Rickard's home lot, and on the 21st of the same month transferred it to his brother Jeremiah, who sold it on the 30th of the same month to Daniel Abbott.[2]

The present owners of the western front of the home lot are Robert H. I. Goddard, Elizabeth A. Shepard, John Carter Brown estate, and Elizabeth A. Gammell, wife of William.

Richard Scott " was admitted a member of the Boston Church, August 28, 1634. He married a sister of the famous Mrs. Hutchinson, and removed with her from Massachusetts. . . . Scott afterwards became a Quaker, and Gov. Hopkins says, the first of that sect in New England. He was one of the early settlers in Providence. The tradition is, that his wife and daughter, in 1657, were whipped ten lashes in Boston, for visiting a Quaker prisoner there."[3] He received a home lot in Providence, signed the first agreement and the compact of 1640. His name appears on the roll of freemen in Providence in 1655, and in 1666 he served as

1. Deeds I, p. 11.   2. Deeds I, p. 4-12-13.   3. Col. R. I. Hist. Soc'y, Vol. II, p. 113.

Deputy. The home lots of Widow Reeve and Joshua Verin came into his posses-sion, as appears by deed of Charles Dyer to Nathaniel Brown.[1] (See Joshua Verin.)

The home lot of Richard Scott became the property of William Field, as appears by the following record:

"At a Towne meeting Jan. 28th 1677:
  being the Towne's quarter day
  It is granted unto Thomas ffeild. Heire unto William ffeild (Deceased) that he may have his House lotts recorded in our Towne records, he paying the Clerkes ffees. . . . The sayd lotts belonging to ye sd Thomas ffeild are Bounded on the west with the Towne street, on the South with the lott of John ffeild, on the East with the highway or Comon, on the north with the lott of George Ricketts now in the possession of the sayd Thomas ffeild and partly with the land of Chad Browne now in the possession of Daniel Abbott."[2] Richard Scott died previous to May 27, 1685.

The present owners of the western front of the home lot of Richard Scott are the Rhode Island Hospital Trust Company and the Joseph Balch estate.

William Field signed the compact of 1640, and in 1647 was appointed on a committee to form a plan of government. He was Assistant for a number of years, 1650, and from 1658 to 1665, and Commissioner from 1656 to 1663. The Fields "were among the early planters, and for long among the chief landholders of the town. 'Fields' Point' is a memorial of one of the first members of the family."[3]

The house of William Field stood a little east of where the Providence Bank now is, and was occupied as a "Garrison house during Philip's war." "It was one of the largest houses of that time, and when the town gave leave to the citizens to 'fortify' themselves, this, with other of the strongest buildings, was 'fortified' with iron gratings at the windows. This, with the other places of security, which the Indians did not venture to attack, saved that part of the town from the con-

1. Deeds II, pp. 300–302.
2. Record of Town Meetings, Book III, p. 5.
3. Planting and Growth of Providence, p. 36.

flagration of March, 1676. . . . The 'Garrison house' remained until 1772. It stood about forty or fifty feet from the Town street. The last of the original owners of the site sold it in that year (Feb., 1772,) to Joseph Brown, who in the year 1774 built there the house now owned by the Providence Bank."[1] The home lot adjoining him on the north (Richard Scott's) became his and was, with the original home lot of William Field, after his decease, transferred by the town, January 28, 1677, to his heir, Thomas Field. (See Richard Scott.)

The present owners of the western front of the home lot of William Field are the Providence National Bank and the Providence Institution for Savings.

John Field "removed from Bridgewater to Providence soon after its settlement." He received a home lot and signed the first agreement and the compact of 1640.

"Whereas there is a highway [now Crawford street.] lieing from ye Towne streete to ye side (or to say the salt water) the which lieth against ye house lot which formerly belonged to John Field. The which lot is now in ye possession of ye heirs of Gideon Crawford. Recorded Feb. 2, 1708-9."[2]

This home lot was in the possession of Gideon Crawford, May 7, 1691. (See Joshua Winsor.)

The present owners of the western front of the home lot of John Field are the heirs of Isaac Brown and the heirs of Rufus Greene.

Joshua Winsor came from the borough of Windsor, England. He received a home lot, and signed the first agreement and the compact of 1640. "Five of the descendants of his only son Samuel, all of the name of Winsor, were settled Baptist ministers within the State of Rhode Island."

May 7, 1691 :

"I, Samuel Winsor, . . . of Providence . . . for a valuable consideration . . . have sold . . . unto Gideon Crawford a home lott in the

1. Planting and Growth of Providence, p. 37.   2. Deeds I, p. 55.

Town of Providence known by ye name of Shepard's lott which lott in the original was my father Joshua Winsor's but since in consideration of Keeping the Antientt man it became mine, which is in Estimation four or five acres be it more or less. It being bounded on ye south with ye land now in ye possession of Thomas Field, on ye west with a Highway fronting against the salt river, on the north with the land of ye said Crawford, and on ye east with a highway."[1]

The western front of the home lot of Joshua Winsor is now owned by Elizabeth S. Howard and Henry J. Steere.

Thomas Harris "was received a purchaser of Providence previous to Aug. 20, 1637. He was brother to William Harris. He left a will which was proved July 20, 1686." He signed the first agreement and the compact of 1640 and was appointed Commissioner from Providence for a number of years, and was a member of the Committee appointed February 19, 1665, to run the seven-mile line. His home lot was the property of Thomas Field, May 7, 1691. (See Joshua Winsor.)

The western part of the home lot of Thomas Harris is now owned by Henry J. Steere.

Adam Goodwin signed the compact of 1640 and received a home lot.

" The 1st of January 1648 (so called) Adam Goodwin sold unto Richard Osbon all his right in Providence both housing and all other Privileges, only the said Richard Osbon hath granted Adam Goodwin the house and yard during his wife's life, only the said Adam Goodwin is to repair it."[2]

" 27th of the 5th month [July] 1650 (called).

" Richard Osborne sold unto Thomas Harris the house and house lot which the said Richard Osborne bought of Adam Goodwin, only the said Adam Goodwin's wife shall have liberty to dwell in the said house according to the agreement made and reserved at first by the said Adam."[3]

1. Deeds II, p. 112.   2. Trans., p. 77.   3. Trans., p. 125.

7

February 12, 1702–3:

Adam Goodwin's home lot "formerly belonged unto Thomas Harris, Senr."[1] and on the 20th of November, 1728, it was owned by William Field and Robert Gibbs. (See William Burrows.)

The western front of the home lot of Adam Goodwin is now in the possession of the heirs of Ezra W. Howard and Elizabeth S. Howard.

William Burrows received a home lot and signed the compact of 1640.

At a Town Meeting, October the 12th, 1663:

"Ordered that the Town deputies shall go to all the Inhabitants belonging unto this Town, see what will be freely contributed towards the relief of William Burrows: and if a considerable sum cannot be granted in that way for them to make Report unto the Town and for the Town to levy a rate upon the inhabitants for the relief of the said William Burrows."[2]

January 28, 1705–6:

"An account of what land belongs to John and Mary Lapham in Providence on the East side of the seven mile line. ffirst, Two Lotts in the Towne, namely, the Lotts of William Mann & William Burrows."[3]

"Articles of partition and quitclaim made this 20th day of November, A. D. 1728, . . . between John Lapham and Nicholas Lapham both of Dartmouth . . . possessed by deeds of Gift from our Honored father John Lapham, deceased. . . . First the said John Lapham is to have the two home lots in the Town, called six acre Lotts Lieing betwixt the Land belonging to the Heirs of Daniel Williams, deceased, and that which was the homestead land of Thomas Harris, deceased, now in possession of William Field and Robert Gibbs."[4]

The house in which the capture of the Gaspee was planned was located on the home lot of William Burrows, at the corner of South Main and Planet streets. The following in regard to the preparation for this expedition, and the location of the house, is an abbreviated transcript from the account given in the Rhode Island Colonial Records, Vol. VII, p. 69, 70:

1. Trans., p. 373.   2. Trans., p. 167.   3. Deeds II, p. 25.   4. Deeds VII, p. 424.

"John Brown, one of the first and most respectable merchants of Providence resolved on the destruction of the Gaspee, and directed one of his trusty ship-masters to collect eight of the largest long boats in the harbor, and to place them, at Fenner's wharf, directly opposite to the dwelling of Mr. James Sabin. This house, then unfinished, was occupied as an inn. It was soon after purchased and completed by Welcome Arnold, who resided there till his death, in 1798. It then became the residence of his eldest son, Samuel G. Arnold, and subsequently of his son, Richard J. Arnold, who altered and enlarged it materially. The house is on the east side of South Main street, on the northeast corner of Planet street."

The present owner of the western front of the home lot of William Burrows is the Providence Institution for Savings.

William Mann received a home lot and signed the compact of 1640. His home lot in 1705–6 was owned by John and Mary Lapham. (See William Burrows.)

The western part of the home lot is now owned by the Arnold Estate Company, Elizabeth B. Updike, Mrs. Charles H. Henshaw, Mrs. Reginald Howe, and A. B. Adams.

William Wickenden removed from Salem, and was received a purchaser at Providence, before August 20, 1637. He signed the first agreement, also the compact of 1640, and is named in the deed of confirmation. He was one of the first Commissioners from Providence, a member of the Town Council in 1651, a member of the Committee appointed to form a plan of government in 1647, and a member of the Committee appointed in April, 1661, to run the boundary line. "He was colleague with Chad Brown, in the pastoral charge of the Baptist Church at Providence," and "was at one time in New York, where, it is said, he preached and was imprisoned for it about four months. He died Feb. 23, 1670,"[1]

1. Col. R. I, Hist. Soc'y, Vol. II, p. 109.

"The 21ˢᵗ September 1646.

"William Wickenden sold unto Christopher Unthank his house and home lot excepting two pole square of Ground on the south corner next the street [Power street] which Nathaniel Dickens now possesseth."[1]

"27ᵗʰ 11ᵗʰ Month 1650.

"Mr. Throckmorton sold unto Mr. Sayles the house and lot which was Nathaniel Dickens, which Mr. ——— bought of Mr. Ralph Earle formerly belonging to William Wickenden."[2]

May 12, 1652:

John Sailes "bought of William Wickenden, '2 poles square lying at the south side of Mr. Sayles new home lot next unto the highway.'"[3]

March 28, 1664–5:

"Upon the request of Daniel Williams it is granted unto him to make use of the highway, [now Power street] lying between Mr. Sailes lot and Jane Power's lot, and upon the same conditions as Mr. Sailes formerly used the same."[4]

The home lot of William Wickenden in 1728 "belonged to the heirs of Daniel Williams, deceased." (See William Mann.)

The present owners of the western front of the home lot of William Wickenden are E. Bigelow Adams and the West Providence Land Company.

Nicholas Power received a home lot and signed the compact of 1640. He died August 25, 1657, intestate, and on the 27th of May, 1667, the Town Council made his will and disposed of his estate. His home lot became the property of his widow, Jane.

The western front of the home lot of Nicholas Power is now in the possession of Cornelia C. Greene, the heirs of Rhoda Steere, and John W. Smith, trustee.

1. Trans., p. 76.   3. Narragansett Hist. Reg., Vol. II, p. 293.
2. Ibid, p. 125.   4. Trans., p. 171.

Joane Tiler received a home lot and signed the compact of 1640.

" 26th day of May, 1663:

"I, John Sayles of Providence . . . for a valuable sum of money paid unto me by William Hawkins inhabitant of ye Towne aforesaid . . . have . . . sould unto ye said William Hawkins . . . ye right which I bought of Ralph Earle, which he bought of Nathaniel Dickens, which formerly belonged unto Joane Tiler afterwards wife unto ye said Nathaniel Dickens."[1]

" 27. 5 mo. 1650:

" Nathaniel Dickens sold unto Nicholas Power his home lot lying next to Widow Sayles her home lot."[2]

The present owners of the western front of the home lot of Joane Tiler are Julia Bullock and John W. Smith, trustee.

Jane Sears received a home lot and signed the compact of 1640. This home lot came into the possession of Daniel Williams, son of Roger, as appears by the will of Daniel, made on the 9th of May, 1712, five days before his death, by which he gives to his son, Roger Williams, his homestead, a home lot on the town street, bounded on the south with the lot of William Hopkins, and on the north with the lot of Nicholas Power, [originally the home lot of Joane Tiler,] with a dwelling house, etc.; "provided he disturb not his mother Rebekah Williams of her reasonable privilege and benefit in said dwelling house and premises during her natural life."[3] To his daughter Patience he gave a home lot on the Town Street [originally Edward Hart's] that he bought of Richard and Ann Waterman, October 30, 1698, bounded by the lot of William Hopkins on the north, and the lot of Samuel Winsor on the south, and described as near the salt water at the south end of the town.[4]

The western front of the home lot of Jane Sears is now the property of the heirs of William Thayer, Marcy A. and Julia Earle, and the heirs of George Earle.

1. Deeds, No. 1, p. 30.   3. Deeds A X, 311.
2. Deeds, &c., Trans., p. 125. 4. Deeds XIX, 506.

Thomas Hopkins was born in England, April 7, 1616. He received a home lot in Providence, and signed the compact of 1640. He was a member of the church at Providence. He was appointed Commissioner for a number of years, and was a member of the Town Council in 1667 and 1672. He died at Little-worth, Oyster Bay, Long Island, in 1684, at the residence of his daughter-in-law, Elizabeth. His home lot became the property of his son William.

The western front of the home lot of Thomas Hopkins is now owned by Sarah A. Congdon and Lydia A. Godfrey.

Edward Hart received a home lot and signed the compact of 1640.

"28. 1st mo. so called [March] 1679:

Robert West sold all his lands to Resolved Waterman. "His house lot [formerly Edward Hart's home lot,] four acres, . . . bounded west on street, north by the home lot of Thomas Hopkins, east by highway, south by home lot of Joshua Winsor."[1]

October 30, 1698:

"I, Richard Waterman, . . . have sold . . . to Daniel Williams . . . one house lot in Providence joining to the Lott of Samuel Winsor on the South and the lot of William Hopkins on the North . . . with an old house and orchard being upon it."[2]

This home lot was, in 1712, given by will of Daniel Williams to his daughter Patience. (See Jane Sears.)

The western front of the home lot of Edward Hart is now owned by Ellen Lynch and the heirs of George B. Earle.

Mathew Weston. "The 20th of May, 1643. It was agreed by the General [people] that Mathew Wesson shall have that home share of Ground which lieth between Robert Wash [West] and John Lippitt also that he shall have three Acres

1. Deeds I, p. 88.   2. Deeds XIX, p. 506.

of Meadow Ground where he think it most convenient which is not already laid out, but if the said Mathew Weson be absent from the Town above eighteen Months being neither Wife nor child here, the aforesaid land shall fall into the Towns Hand again."[1]

" 27th[th] 5th mo. 1650 (called)

" Ordered . . . that Joshua Winsor shall possess the lot which was formerly Nathan [Mathew] Weston's, provided that the said Joshua Winsor pay unto the town £30 s.15, at the next harvest and 15. at the next after in merchantable pay for to be delivered for Nath. Weston's use."[2]

It appears that Joshua Winsor owned this lot October 9, 1663. " I, Joshua Winsor . . . my lot that is called Mathew Weston's."[3] And that Samuel Winsor was the owner October 30, 1698. (See Edward Hart.")

The western front of Mathew Weston's home lot is now owned by the heirs of George B. Earle.

John Lippitt received a home lot and signed the compact of 1640. He was chosen a member of the Committee appointed to form a plan of government in 1647. He removed to Warwick, his name appearing on the roll of freemen of that town in 1655.

April 27, 1652, John Lippitt sold all his real estate to Arthur Fenner, reserving his home lot.

The western front of the home lot of John Lippitt is now owned by Mary F. Gladding, the heirs of James H. Prendergast, and Burnet S. W. Bragunn.

Hugh Bewit, "in Dec. 1640 was banished from Massachusetts. He was found guilty of heresy, and that his person and errors are dangerous for the infection of others. He was ordered for this to be gone out of our jurisdiction by the 24th inst. upon pain of death, and not to return upon pain of being hanged."[4]

---

1. Trans., p. 73. 3. Trans., p. 27.
2. Trans., p. 142. 4. Col. R. I. Hist. Soc'y, Vol. II, p. 118.

Upon removing to Providence he received a grant of land, signed the compact of 1640, and became a member of the church. He was appointed to the office of Commissioner for a number of years, and also served as General Sergeant and Solicitor General.

"27th 11th mo. 1644.

"Hugh Bewit sold unto William Hawkins his home share of land bounding on the North with the land of John Lippitt on the South with the land of the said William Hawkins [formerly the home lot of Robert West] on the east and west with the common."[1]

"27th 11th mo. 1644.

"Hugh Bewit sold unto the general People of the Towne of Providence his house and home share of ground [the home lot of Ezekiel Holliman] bounding upon the land of Richard Waterman on the North, on the land of Stukely Westcott on the South on the east with the common on the west with the highway."[2]

"27th 11th mo. 1650."

Hugh Bewit sold to Richard Waterman the home lot last above described.

Pardon Tillinghast was in possession of the home lot of Hugh Bewit in 1681, as appears by the following statement:

"In ye yeare 1681. When I William Hopkins of Providence was their surveyor did then lay out unto Edward London one Lott [a warehouse lot] above high water marke by ye water side containing 30 foote square. It being laid out four poles distant from Pardon Tillinghast his home lott which he bought of William Hawkins Senr. [originally Hugh Bewit's]. The which said lott is layed out with the like privileges as others of the like qualitie have allowed them to the water.

"Given under my hand this 29th day of March 1686

WILLIAM HOPKINS."[3]

1. Trans., p. 74.   2. Trans., p. 75.   3. Deeds I, p. 137.

The above mentioned Pardon Tillinghast received a "free grant of Twenty-five acres of land the 19th of 11th mo. 1645," (Jan. 19, 1646.) He succeeded Thomas Olney as pastor of the Baptist Church, and "at his own expense built the first meeting-house about the year 1700." "This house was situated on the west side of North Main street, nearly opposite Star street. In 1711, Mr. Tillinghast, in consideration of the love and good will he bore the church over which he was then pastor, executed to them and their successors in the same faith and order, a deed of the meeting house and the lot on which it stood."[1] He died January 29, 1717–18.

By will, dated December 15, 1715, he disposed of his home lot as follows:

"I give to my son Joseph my Present Dwelling house and home Lott with all the privileges pertaining thereunto after his mother's decease to be to him and his heirs forever."[2]

The Tillinghast burial ground was located on the home lot where it still remains undisturbed near the northwest corner of Transit and Benefit streets.

The Church of the Saviour, located on the home lot of Hugh Bewit, at the corner of Benefit and Transit streets, was built in 1840 by the "Corporation of St. Stephen's Church," and occupied by them until 1862, when they removed to their present place of worship on George street. The St. Stephen's Church was organized in 1838, and the corner-stone of their first place of worship was laid, on the 15th day of April, 1840.[3]

The western front of the home lot of Hugh Bewit is now owned by Cornelius O'Leary and William McElroy.

Robert West received a home lot and signed the compact of 1640. In 1644 this home lot was in the possession of Williams Hawkins. (See Hugh Bewit.)

The home lot originally assigned to Edward Hart came into the possession of Robert West, and was by him sold "28th 1st mo. 1679" (?) to Resolved Waterman. (See Edward Hart.)

1. Annals of Prov., p. 414.   2. Wills II, p. 25.   3. From Mr. George T. Hart.

8

Robert West, in 1644, received £5 bounty for killing two wolves.

The western front of the home lot of Robert West is now owned by Philip A. Munroe and Hugh and Dennis Gorman.

William Hawkins received a home lot and signed the compact of 1640. He " stayed and went not away " during King Philip's war, and was one of those to whom land in Narragansett was granted by the Assembly in 1677. He also came into possession of the two home lots next north of his, namely, Robert West's, in 1644, and Hugh Bewit's; also the home lot of Joane Tiler. He was an early member of the Church in Providence.

" 2nd day Feb. 1673.

" I, William Hawkins . . . Have freely given . . . unto my son William Hawkins . . . two house lots or home shares of land with all ye housing, fencing and fruit trees standing and being upon ye said land . . . The which said lotts or home shares of land . . . being in ye Row of house lotts . . . Bounding on ye Westerne side with ye highway or Towne streete & on ye Eastern end with a highway . . . Bounding on ye Southern side with a house lot or home share of land of Thomas Roberts of ye aforesaid towne of Providence and on ye Northern side with a house lot or home share of land of James Ashton formerly inhabitant . . . of Providence."[1]

The western front of the home lot of William Hawkins is now owned by Mrs. George M. Geehard, John Baker, of East Providence, and William W. Rickard.

Christopher Unthank received a home lot and signed the compact of 1640. June 1, 1663:

" I, Christoper Unthank now of Warwick, . . . weaver, . . . upon valuable consideration in hand already received . . . have sold unto Thomas Roberts of Providence . . . about the year 1658 . . . my house and house lot which did belong to me in Providence, together with a parcel of land lying

---

1. Deeds I, p. 82.

beyond the Runnet in the sd lott which belongeth to Robert Williams his house lot which I bought of the said Robert Williams, together with all the appurtenances belonging to either, together with all my right & Privileges in all the commons . . . All which parcels of land with my house aforesaid are bounded on the south with that lot which at present Thomas Sucklin possesseth, on the north with the land of William Hawkins on the East with the Common & on the West with the highway next to ye sea. . . . Only that parcel of land specified beyond the Runnet is bounded on the west with the said Runnet, on the south with the highway & on the East with the common on the North with that parcel of land which my house stood upon which is the home lot before specified."[1]

The western front of the home lot of Christopher Unthank is now owned by Horace C. Tallman, Mrs. Daniel J. Farrar, and William McElroy.

Robert Williams, who is said to have been a brother of Roger Williams, received a home lot and signed the compact of 1640. In 1648 he was appointed one of the first Commissioners from Providence; he was Commissioner for 1651–2; in 1655, member of the Town Council; in 1664, Justice of the Peace, and General Solicitor in 1673–74.

27th 8th mo. [Oct.] 1644:

Robert Williams purchased of Robert Morris the home lot of Daniel Abbott which he sold Oct. 1, 1665 to Daniel Abott, Jr. (See Daniel Abbott.)

June 1, 1663:

He sold his original home lot to Christopher Unthank. (See Chris. Unthank.)

Feb. 8, 1664–5:

"Robert Williams of Newport schoolmaster . . . sold to . . . John Scott of Providence . . . his dwelling house in Providence, with ye housing, home share and orchard as I bought them of William Reynolds."

The western front of the home lot of Robert Williams is now in the possession of the heirs of Lydia J. Stillwell, the Mariners' Bethel, and the heirs of William Bradley.

1. Deeds II, p. 65.

Plan showing the
Original Water Line
ON THE WEST SIDE OF
Providence River.

COPYRIGHT BY CHARLES W. HOPKINS.
1886.

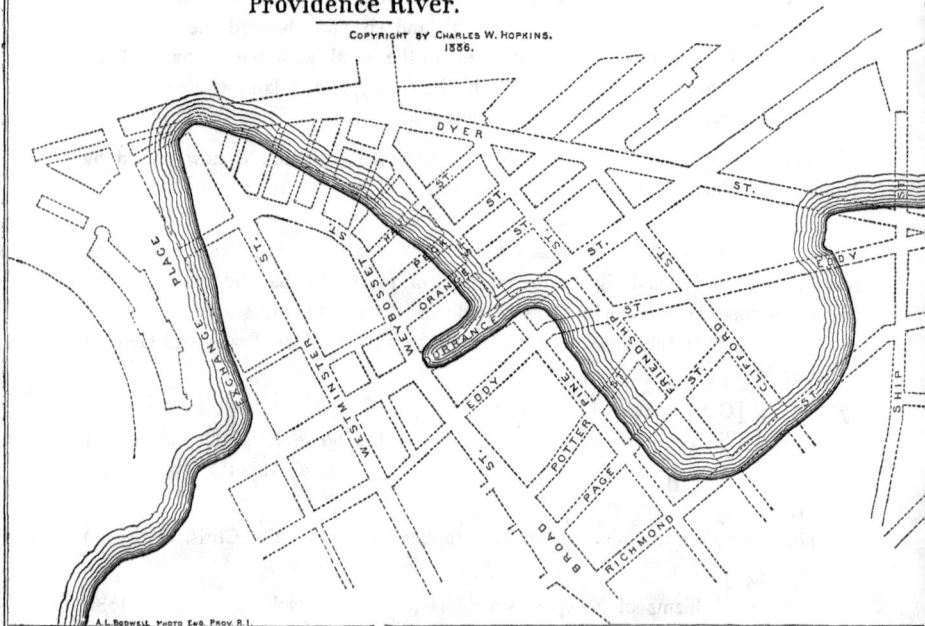

DYER

ST.

WESTMINSTER ST.

WEYBOSSET ST.

ORANGE ST.

EXCHANGE PLACE

FRIENDSHIP ST.

PINE ST.

POTTER ST.

PAGE

EDDY ST.

BROAD

RICHMOND

CLIFFORD ST.

EDDY

SHIP

ST.

ST.

ST.

ST.

ST.

EDDY

ALLENS · AVE ·

RICHMOND

ST.

ST.

MANCHESTER

HENDERSON

CHESTNUT

SOUTH

PARSONAGE POINT

ELM

CRARY

ST.

LANGLEY

ST.

BORDEN

ST.

LOCKWOOD

ST.

ST.

HOSPITAL

APPENDIX.

ORIGINAL OWNERS

OF THE

PROVIDENCE PLANTATIONS.

(See Introduction, page VII.)

Ann^d 1660

Presented for avoyding (so much as may be) future
Contention

A revised List (saving Correction, with Addition) of Lands
and Meddows, As they were orriginally Lotted, ffrom the
beginning of the Plantation of Providence, in the Nar-
regansetts Bay in New England, unto the (then) Inhabitants of the said Plantation, until Ann^d 16

[*Illegible.*]   ordered by the Inhabitants of the Towne for Composing the
Orriginal List.

Home-Lots

Begining at Mile-End-Cove

Robert Williams.
Christopher Unthanks.
William Hawkings.
Robert West.
Hugh Bewitt.
John Lippett.
Matthew Wesson.
Edward Harte.
Thomas Hopkings.
Widdow Sayers.
Widdow Tylers.
Nicholas Powers.
A high Way
William Wickenden.
William Man.
William Barrows.
Adam Goodings.
Thomas Harris.
Joshua Winsor.
John ffeild.
William ffeild.
Richard Scotte.
Georg Ricketts.
John Warnner.
Chade Browne.
Daniell Abbott.
William Reinolds
Stutlow Wescoate
Ezekiel Hollyman

Richard Waterman.
ffrancis Wessons.
Thomas Angells.
Thomas Olnye.
Robert Cole.
A high Way
William Carpender.
John Sweet.
Alice Daniell.
William Harris.
John Throckmorton.
Joshua Vearing.
Widdow Reeve.   [Torn.]
John Smith.
John Greene Senior.
Thomas James.
William Arnold.
Francis Weekes.
Benedicte Arnold
John Greene Junior.
Edward Manton
Thomas Painter
Matthew Waller
Grigory Dexter

Over Mooshawsick River

John Smiths home-Lott
where he build a Mille.

Six Acres Lotts

By the River side, beginning at Mile-End-Cove

6 : Acres of William Reinolds.
6 : Acres of ffrancis Weekes.
6 : Acres of John Throckmortons.
6 : Acres of William Arnolds.
6 : Acres of William Carpenders. } Saving high ways
6 : Acres of Benedicte Arnolds. } and Meere-Banckes.
6 : Acres of Edward Copes.
6 : Acres of Roger Williams.
   with What-Cheare.

In-Lands next to John Throckmortons

6 : Acres of William Harris.
6 : Acres of William Wickendens.
6 : Acres of Nicholas Powers.
6 : Acres of William Mans. } Saving high Wayes.
   A high Way
6 : Acres of William Hawkings.

On the North-side of Wanasquatuckett

6 : Acres of William Wickendens
2 : Acres of Grigory Dexters, in pt of
   his 6 : Acre Lott —
6 : Acres of Thomas Hopkings.
6 : Acres of John ffeilds
        Common and a high Way through
6 : Acres of Thomas Angells
6 : Acres of Thomas Olnyes saving high wayes,
6 : Acres of Stutlow Wescoats.

9

By the West-River neere New Bridge

6 : Acres of Robert Williams.
6 : Acres of Joshua Winsors.
6 : Acres of Thomas Harris
     on Mooshausick-River—

At Smale Brooke

60 : Acres of Thomas Angells
60 : Acres of ffrancis Weekes
          Over Smale Brooke

30 : Acres in part of William Arnolds 60 : Acres

Lands and Meddowes Lotted
on Waubosset Side

Begining at Saxafrage, by the Water-Side
Next the Townes-Bounds
A high-Way

25 : Acres to William Arnold, with Meddow
besides Wast Ground, and a high Waye
crosse to Pautuxitt
A high-Way

91 : Acres to Richard Waterman with Meddow.

60 : Acres to Thomas Hopkings.
A high Way

25 : Acres to Nicholas Power in parte of William
Mans 60 : Acres
A high-Way by the side of long-Cove
A high-Way on this side of long-Cove

20 : Acres to Thomas Angell.
A high-Way

25 : Acres to Ezechiel Hollyman, with parte of-
a shaire of Meddowe.

25 : Acres to John Warnner.

05 : Acres to William Reinolds, with 3 Acres-
towards the Water side, for his second shaire-
of meddow.

Savinge
high-Ways.

05 : Acres to Roger Williams.
Severall high-ways with wast Ground.

20 : Acres to Robert Williams, over the high-wayes :
Saving (allso) a high-way, by the 5 Acres-Lotts
ffive Acres Lotts lying together

05 : Acres to John Throckmorton.

05 : Acres to Edward Cope.

05 : Acres to ffrancis Weekes.
05 : Acres to Thomas Angell
05 : Acres to Thomas Harris
05 : Acres to Richard Scotte
　　　　A high-Way
A swampe and the vacant land to
Robert Williams, for his 5 : Acres.
05 : Acres to William Carpender
05 : Acres to Thomas Olnye
05 : Acres to Thomas James
05 : Acres to William ffeild
　　　　A high-Way .
05 : Acres to John ffeild
05 : Acres to Chade Browne
05 : Acres to Daniell Abbott
05 : Acres to Adam Goodings
05 : Acres to Widdow Tyler
05 : Acres to Widdow Sayers
　　　　A high-Way
05 : Acres to Christopher Unthanks
05 : Acres to Edward Heart
　　　　A high Way crossing the River
05 : Acres to Stutlow Wescoate
05 : Acres to Benedicte Arnold, saving
　　　a highway by Solentary-hill wch. is Common
04 : Acres to Benedict Arnold in part
　　　of his 20 : Acres.
A crosse high Way
05 : Acres to Thomas Hopkings.
05 : Acres to Nicholas Powers.
05 : Acres to William Wickenden
　　　　Saving high way
Halfe Acre to Joshua Winsor in
parte of his 5 : Acres.
　　　　A high Way
03 : Acres to Joshua Winsor in parte
　　　of his 5 : Acres.
05 : Acres to William Hawkings
04 : Acres to Grigory Dexter in parte
　　　of his 6 : Acres.

A Meere-Bank on the Plaine
One Acre and halfe to Joshua Winsor in rest
of his 5 : Acres—
25 : Acres to William Man.
25 : Acres to Robert West
The Rest Common

In-Land, beginning at Maussaupauoge

150 : Acres between William Arnold—
Benedict Arnold and William Carpender—
Saving highe ways and vacant Land
Vacant Land in posse for John Greene Junio[r]
25 : Acres of Robert Coles ⎫
20 : Acres to William Carpender ⎬ Saving high Wayes
91 : Acres to ffrancis Wesson ⎭ and vacant-land—
60 : Acres to Adam Goodings ⎫ Butting on a Ponde
80 : Acres to Roger Williams ⎭ Saving high wayes.
North-West from the Pondes.

20 : Acres to John Throckmorton ⎫
20 : Acres to Edward Cope—and his second ⎪
shaire of meddow ⎪
Common about halfe a mile ⎬ Saving high wayes.
60 : Acres of Robert West ⎪
35 : Acres of William Mans ⎪
60 : Acres of William Wickendens ⎭
The Towne Bounds with Common

In-Land by Waunasquetuckett, On the hether
Plaine, adjoyning unto Robert Williams 20 : Acres

20 : Acres of ffrancis Weekes ⎫
20 : Acres of Richard Scotts ⎬ Saving high wayes.

60 : Acres divided in 20 Acres a peece- ⎫
   To William Harris, Thomas Harris ⎬ Saving high wayes
     and Widdow Sayers ⎭
          Common

80 : Acres to John ffeild ⎫
20 : Acres to Daniell Abbott ⎬ Saving high wayes
20 : Acres to Stutlow Wescoate ⎪
    betwext the plaines ⎭

        On the further Plaine

---

60 : Acres to Grigorye Dexter saving
    high wayes

20 : Acres to Thomas Hopkings ⎫
20 : Acres to Adam Goodings ⎬ Saving high wayes
20 : Acres to Nicholas Powers ⎭

20 : Acres to William Wickenden ⎫
20 : Acres to William ffield ⎬ Saving high wayes
16 : Acres to Benedicte Arnold in ⎪
    the rest of his 20 : Acres ⎭

20 : Acres to Joshua Winsor ⎫
20 : Acres to Thomas James ⎬ Saving high wayes
20 : Acres to Widdow Tyler ⎭

        Beyond the Plaine

---

85 : Acres to Edward Manton, saving
    high-ways

        Neerer the River

---

60 : Acres to Daniell Abbott, saving
    high wayes

        Neerer Pauchassett

---

25 : Acres to William Barrowes, saving
    high wayes

        Vacant-Lands

Meddowes

Beginning by the River-Side, on this side
Pautuxette-ffalls
Robert Coles, ffirst Shaire of his Meddowes
Parte of Thomas Angells first Shaire
Parte of Ezechiel Hollymans first Shaire
ffrancis Wessons first Shaire
Thomas James first Shaire
William Carpenders first Shaire
Parte of Richard Watermans first Shaire
The other parte of Ezekiel Hollymans first Shaire
Roger Williams ffirst Shaire
Parte of John Throckmortons first Share
A high-way with Waubosset Common
Another parte of John Throckmortons first Shaire
The other parte of Richard Watermans first Shaire
A Cove and little Island for halfe an Acre of
Chade Brownes first Shaire
Part of William Reinolds first Shaire
The other parte of John Throckmortons first Shaire
John Greene Senio.ʳ his ffirst Shaire
Joshua Vearinges first Shaire
William Harris first Shaire
Parte of Thomas Olnyes first Shaire
In-Land Meddowes beginning at Mausaupauogg
Pond

Robert Wests second Shaire
William Wickendens second Shaire
Daniel Abbotts first Shaire on Spectacle Pond
William Mans second Shaire
Meaddowes at Paushausett River

Edward Hearts first Shaire

Christopher Unthanks first Shaire
Thomas Hopkings first Shaire
Widow Sayers first Shaire
William ffeilds first Shaire.

Inland meddowes upon the same River

John Lippetts second Shaire
Joshua Winsors second Shaire
Chade Brownes second Shaire
Roger Williams second Shaire by
    the five Trees.

On the hither Side of Paushausett River.

Hugh Bewitts first Shaire
William Barrowes first Shaire.

ffrom the River of Waunasquetuckett

Halfe of Edward Mantons second Shaire
Edward Mantons ffirst Shaire
William Mans ffirst Shaire
Robert Wests ffirst Shaire
The other halfe of Edward Mantons second Shaire
Daniel Abbotts second Shaire.

Neerer Waunasquetuckett River.

Stutlow Wescoats first Shaire
Benedicte Arnolds first Shaire.

Meddowes On the Townes Side

Beginning at Waunasquetuckett River
An other parte in parcells of Thomas Olnyes Meddowes
William Arnolds first Shaire
Other parcells of Thomas Olnyes Meddowes
Matthew Wallers Swampe for his second Shaire
An other Part ⎫
An other Part ⎬ of Thomas Olnyes Meddowes
The other Part of William Reinolds first Shaire with
   An Island
                   At Smale Brooke

Thomas Hopkings second Shaire
William Hawkings second Shaire
Grigorye Dexters second Shaire
ffrancis Weekes second Shaire
                   Over Samale Brooke

Grigorye Dexters first Shaire
John ffeilds   Shaire
         Upon Maushausett River, on the Necke Side

Part of Thomas Harris second Shaire
Part of ffrancis Weekes first Shaire
Part of Richard Scotts first Shaire
The other part of Thomas Angells first Shaire
The other part of Richard Scotts first Shaire
William Wickendens first Shaire
                   At the Greate Meddowe

John ffeilds first Shaire
John Warnners first Shaire
Thomas Harris second Shaire — in pt.

Christopher Unthanks first Shaire
Widdow Tylers first Shaire
John Throckmortons second Shaire
Thomas Olnyes second Shaire
John Greenes Junio.ͤ first Shaire
                    Meddowe Common
Widdow Sayers second Shaire
                    Meddowe Common
            On the West Side

                Meddowe Common
Nicholas Powers second Shaire
John Greene Senio.ͤ his second Shaire
John Smith 5 Acres and $\frac{3}{4}$ in case he
        builde a Mill
Adam Goodings second Shaire
John Smith 3 : Acres and $\frac{1}{4}$ in case he
        builde a Mill
Nicholas Powers first Shaire
Adam Goodings first Shaire
William ffeilds first Shaire
Joshua Winsors first Shaire
The other part of Chade Brownes first Shaire
Edward Copes first Shaire
                On the West River

Thomas Angells second Shaire
Christopher Unthanks second Shaire
Widdow Tylers second Shaire
        South-Side on the West River

Robert Williams two Shaires
William Barrows second Shaire
The other part of Thomas Harris second Shaire
        The other part of ffrancis Weekes Meddow
            upon Pautuckett River.

INDEX.

11

www.ingramcontent.com/pod-product-compliance
Lightning Source LLC
Chambersburg PA
CBHW070929270326
41927CB00011B/2780